Magickal Protection

Harnessing the Power of Protection Magick, Archangels, Angels, Angelic Sigils, Magical Rituals, and Spells for Psychic Self-Defense, along with a Guide to Enochian Magic

Your Free Gift (only available for a limited time)

Thanks for getting this book! If you want to learn more about various spirituality topics, then join Mari Silva's community and get a free guided meditation MP3 for awakening your third eye. This guided meditation mp3 is designed to open and strengthen ones third eye so you can experience a higher state of consciousness. Simply visit the link below the image to get started.

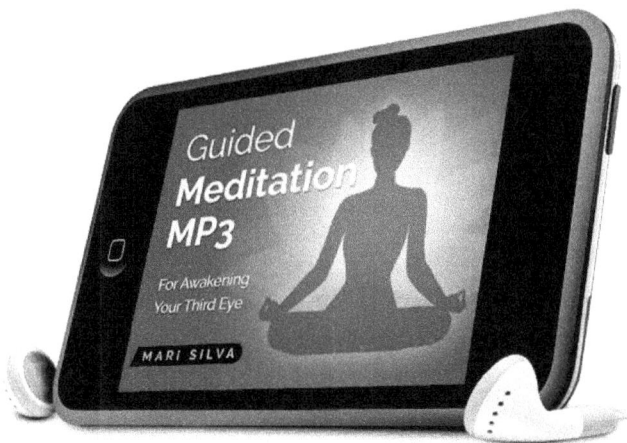

https://spiritualityspot.com/meditation

Table of Contents

Part 1: Protection Magick

The Ultimate Guide to Using Magical Rituals, Spells and Angelic Protection for Psychic Self-Defense

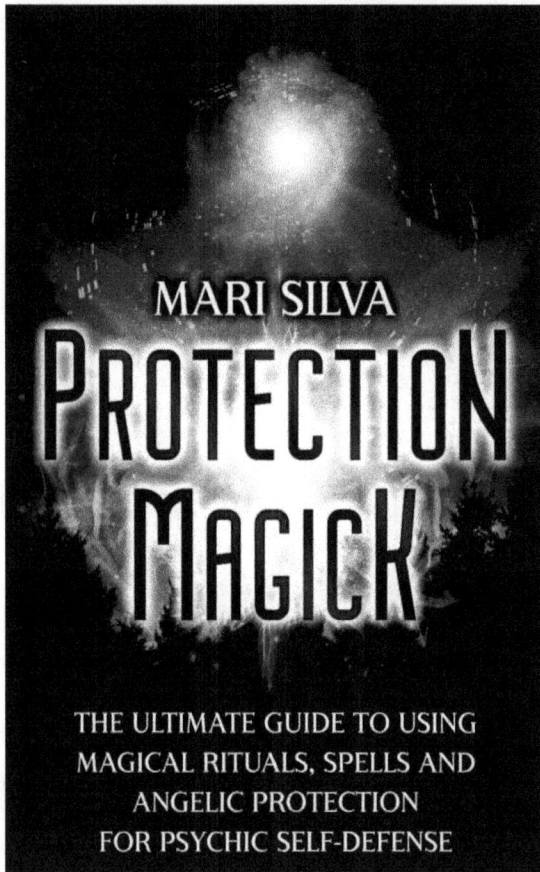

Introduction

You protect your home by purchasing insurance and performing routine maintenance, right? Likewise, you protect yourself against the elements by wearing suitable clothing or sunscreen, and you protect your car with regular maintenance and services.

So, how do you protect *yourself* in normal life? It doesn't matter what aspect of your life you consider. You do stuff to protect it and yourself. So why wouldn't you want to protect yourself when you perform magical work?

Keeping yourself safe is paramount when you carry out magick. You are dealing with forces and energies that are not bound by Earthly rules, so you need to know exactly how to keep danger at bay and be safe in the spiritual realms. Forget what you have seen on TV and in films about magick, witches, supernatural beings, and all things connected to "witchcraft." Instead, learn what it means to be connected to nature and the forces that control our lives. Stop living a mundane life in the shadows and let the elements and planets share their energies with you.

Life is hard, and getting help from the spiritual forces surrounding you will help you live a more satisfying existence. Magick, witchcraft, supernatural forces, call it what you will. It exists, and it is waiting for you to connect with it. If you are already a practitioner of the art, then you will know the importance of protection.

Whether this is your first step into the world of magick or you've been doing it for a while, the information in this book will keep you safe and connected to positive forces.

In today's society, being a witch or performing magick signifies so much more. You are not someone to be afraid of or to be avoided. You are a follower of some of the earth's oldest traditions and practices. You are part of a growing army of individuals looking for measures to save our planet when pollution and environmental crises threaten to ruin it. Let us join forces and embrace all offers of support.

Chapter 1: Protection Magick Basics

When you perform magick work or other types of spells, you are opening yourself up to negative energies and other people's psychic invasions. These types of attacks can range from mildly irritating to outright dangerous. You must protect yourself, your home, and even your children. After all, if you protect them from the "natural world," wouldn't it make sense to protect them from the "supernatural world" as well?

We know how important it is to have protection when exposed to the elements, so consider magick work as just another natural element that requires you to form a shield against its more negative qualities. Think of it as sunscreen for the soul. It doesn't stop everything from getting through, just the harmful rays that can damage you.

Protection magick is one of the oldest forms of magick, dating to the beginning of humanity. All cultures have had some form of protection rituals and charms, some of which are still part of our everyday life. Have you ever broken a mirror and thought, "Oh no, seven years bad luck," or crossed yourself when you see a black cat? Do you toss a pinch of spilled salt over the left shoulder if you spill it? All these customs have deep-rooted origins that relate to protection magick.

There are different categories of protection, and some are defensive while others take a more active role in neutralizing any threat or perpetrator. Most witches don't believe in aggressive forms of protection that involve harming other beings as they follow the adage of "harm none" when performing their art.

Categories of Protective Magick

Preventative magick involves the use of rituals and objects to encourage good luck and fortune for the practitioner. This type of prevention is the very core of magical practice.

Purification magick involves using cleansing to remove harmful or stagnant energies. Washes and baths can remove harm, while the burning of sacred plants creates purifying smoke to dismiss negativity. Sacred oils can also anoint objects with protective properties.

Warding is a type of alarm system setup to warn you when a negative force impacts your life. Hanging crystals, horseshoes, and cinnamon sticks at the entrances to your home will help you keep it cleansed. Wind chimes and wind bells make an attractive form of warding to keep your house free from unfavorable elements.

Boundaries are part of all healthy relationships. When you know your boundaries, you can let yourself be more open and inviting. Setting physical and ethereal boundaries helps to keep your magical and spiritual self safe and fully protected.

Petitioning the deities means offering objects and requests from certain spiritual entities in return for their help. Construct an area to make your offerings in the form of an altar or other focal point to set your intentions. Placing organic matter on your altar creates a spiritual contract that you can enhance with regular offerings and rituals.

Offensive operations, including hexing and cursing, are aggressive and taboo to most practitioners. Try a deflective spell instead or return to sender maneuver to deflect negativity back to its source rather than creating your own negative energy. The witch bottle described below is a perfect way to return harm to the original source when the sender is unknown.

Binding and banishing spells are used to restrict the effect magick has on the victim. Physical acts representing sympathetic magick like binding a cord or hammering a nail represent the protective actions that can keep yourself and others safe. Banishing rituals are used to remove negativity and make room for more positive energies. Practitioners should only perform them when they are at their strongest, both physically and mentally.

Shielding

Visualization is used to create a shield of defense to ward off harmful elements. It is perhaps the simplest form of protection, but it is also one of the most effective. Create a bubble around yourself by taking a deep breath, closing your eyes, and picturing a thick crystallized gel-forming an egg-like surrounding for yourself. This bubble will allow light and positive energy to flow in a while, keeping you safe from negative psychic and mental energies.

Practice grounding and centering yourself on creating more realistic bubbles. Breathing exercises will help, so try these simple exercises to help you feel grounded:

1) Belly breathing is also known as diaphragmatic breathing, and it will help you use your entire lung capacity. Start by sitting in a comfortable position and closing your eyes. Place one hand on your diaphragm and breathe deeply. You will feel your stomach expand and rise. Repeat until you feel your chest and ribs follow suit. Repeat this process twenty times.

2) Pausal breathing is all about recognizing the natural switch from inhaling to exhaling. When you recognize the pause, extend it, and use the time to feel more grounded and centered.

3) Breathe with ohm and feel connected to the earth. Begin with belly breathing but think *ohm* as you inhale and exhale. Repeat this process twenty times.

4) Breathe for the body and mind. Did you know that air inhaled through your right nostril activates the left side of your brain, and air from the left nostril stimulates your right side? Give your brain an injection of energy by breathing deeply through your right nostril while blocking

your left nostril for ten breaths - and then swapping sides for another ten breaths.

Enhance your breathing exercises by using physical activity. Stand with your feet slightly apart and your toes pointing directly forward while your arms are relaxed with open palms. Align your head and shoulders with your spine until you feel completely relaxed. When you inhale, raise your arms over your head and clasp your hands while lifting your heels from the floor. When you exhale, lower your heels and arms until they are in their original position. Visualize the energy as it flows through your body and invigorates you both physically and mentally.

Meditation

As part of your normal routine, you should meditate every day to help cleanse and revitalize your mind and spirit. You wouldn't leave the house without washing your hands, face, or body, so why would you start your day with an unclean aura? Meditation shouldn't be something you fear, and the most basic form could be one of the healthiest practices you try. We all need protection from the world, and meditation arms you with the most effective tools. You can have a pure and cleansed mind with a natural spiritual wall to protect you from even the most harmful energies.

Meditation helps you clear any old memories and negative remnants from your past so you can face the world with a clean slate. Moving on and becoming free from the past can be difficult, and meditation gives you the strength to delve deep into your mental and physical vaults and cleanse yourself. By getting rid of your mental garbage, you reduce your vulnerability to spiritual attacks.

Simple Meditation Technique

To begin, keep in mind that meditation is not about thinking. It's all about allowing thoughts to come to you. It's a technique for slowing down your thoughts and allowing yourself to reach your inner consciousness. You should notice that you are slipping into a deeper state of being. You will eventually achieve a peaceful meditative trance in which the world simply exists and is free of all mental connections.

1) Choose a peaceful, cool place to perform your meditation. Sit upright against a wall and cross your legs. You can listen to soothing music, but most beginners find total silence to be more helpful to their success.

2) Begin with the top of your body and tell all your relevant parts to relax. Start at the head and work your way down to your toes

3) Listen to your breathing. Don't alter your natural breathing patterns. Just take notice of them. Feel the air enter and leave and how the rest of your body is affected by the process. Listen to the noise you make when you breathe. Are you loud, or do you breathe quietly?

4) Focus on your breathing until you feel relaxed and at peace. Now your thoughts should begin to enter your mind of their own volition. You aren't thinking of them, but they appear because you are in a state to welcome them. A mind is a wonderful machine, and it will decide what you need to see and what you need to let go of. Acknowledge their presence and then decide what to do with them.

5) Keep repeating step 4 until you feel you have completed your meditation for that day. Each meditation will be different and have varying results. You may experience a trance-like feeling, or you may just feel extremely relaxed. Accept that this is the process, and you will soon feel the benefits. Remember, your mind isn't going to withhold information, but your consciousness may. It is trying to protect you from your inner negativity while your mind realizes you need to let it go. Meditation allows your consciousness to feel safe and be part of the process.

Witch Bottle or Bag

If you prefer your protection to be more tangible, then a witch's bottle or bag may suit your needs.

Take a small jar with a lid, a preserving jar that works well, and place some sharp rusty objects in it. Pins, needles, and nails work well, but anything old, sharp, and past its best will do. Fill the jar halfway, and then add liquid. If you want really strong protection, you can pee in the jar to truly personalize your witch's bottle or if that's too gross for you, use salty water instead. Sea salt works best, but you can use iodized table salt. Seal the jar with wax, red or black are the most effective for repelling negativity, and then choose a place to bury it—the further away from your home, the better. Dig six inches deep and then place the jar in the ground. Cover and return home.

The witch bag is a similar concept, but it's designed to be worn on you, so don't even think about peeing on it! Take a small bag or pouch made from fabric and fill it with positive items like crystals or stones to attract positive energies. Lodestone and amber are lucky and if you have access to a small fossil, place it in the bag as well. Add some dried herbs like rosemary, angelica, or sandalwood, and sprinkle the bag with clove oil for added protection. Wear your bag around your neck or keep it in your pocket for spiritual safeguarding.

Stakeout to Protect Your Home

Boundaries around your home will help you keep it spiritually clean and free from harm. You can personalize your boundaries with personal messages and instructions. Write messages on some iron stakes (available at Home Depot stores) or railroad stakes. "This is my home, and anyone who attempts to invade it will suffer" or simply "Keep out if you mean me harm" - both work, but you should have fun with your personalization.

Use runes or sigils to decorate your stakes and make them stronger once you have completed your messaging. Drive the stakes around the perimeter of your home. You have now created the perfect spiritual boundary and made your home safe and protected.

Back up your boundaries by using eggshell powder to form a protective line at the entrance to your home. The eggshell powder has been used for generations by people who practice Hoodoo and Santeria, and it is traditionally referred to as cascarilla powder. You can make it by collecting eggshells, using ones from your kitchen, or collecting them from the wild. After you've cleaned them, put them in the oven at a low temperature for around 20 minutes at about 300 degrees. You don't want them to be burned; you want them to be dry and brittle.

Grind the shells in a coffee grinder or with an old-fashioned pestle and mortar to make the powder. Scatter the powder where needed, or use some chalk to write your intentions for a fun alternative. Mix three parts shell powder with one part flour and one part hot water. You will have a thick sticky paste that you can shape into sticks by hand and wrap in paper towels for a couple of days to dry thoroughly.

Protect Your Children

You may use basic objects to keep your children safe in the same way you protect your home. Make their everyday toys protective talismans by sprinkling blessed oils or dried lavender in their teddy bear's stuffing. Children will be enchanted if you imbue a toy with a protective chant. When tucking them down with their beloved toy bear, consider a simple yet effective saying like "The magick in this teddy bear will keep the bad things out of here."

Make a sweet dream pillow by filling it with lavender and thyme and adorning it with your child's favorite images. Make the pillow customized for your child by attaching butterflies and colored trim, and then write a nighttime mantra that is just theirs. "Sleep will come with this pillow, and my sweet dreams will take flight."

Magical Tools

Formal ritual magick requires tools, and these can be physically practical or symbolic. There are no hard and fast rules when it comes to the tools you need. The items listed below are far from comprehensive. Still, they will give you an idea of what most practitioners have in their arsenal of magick.

You can use household items, but most practitioners will tell you that the best results are from tools used solely for your magick work. A knife that cuts your vegetables in the kitchen can be used in rituals, but it needs purifying. Keeping your magick tools solely for rituals and spells saves time and endows them with special instructions. Keep all your tools wrapped in natural fabrics and in a sacred space for the best results.

Some practitioners tell dark tales about the need to destroy tools when their owner passes away. This is just an urban myth, and some of the most powerful tools have been handed down through generations.

The Athame

The Athame is a ceremonial knife that traditionally has a double-edged silver-colored blade with a black handle and represents the element of Air. It should be placed in the Eastern sector of your altar to attract positive energies. In rituals, it is used to draw a pentagram sign in the air and direct power to the intended recipient. The athame can discharge the excess energy to the ground once the ritual is completed.

The Bell

The bell is a decorative piece that should not be used excessively in your magick. It should be kept in the north of your altar, as it represents the element of Earth. It is rung nine times at the beginning and the end of rituals and is made of crystal or brass. The number nine is a magical number that denotes completion and perfection.

The Cauldron

In less formal rituals, a metal cauldron can be used to replace your altar, and if it's flameproof, it can also be used to prepare potions and boil herbs outside for a special occasion. A cauldron is not something that every practitioner owns, but it is a practical item that brings the sense of domestic life into the world of magick. You can fill it with flowers or fragrant herbs when it's not in use. The cauldron symbolizes the fifth element of the Spirit.

The Chalice

This instrument is a ritual cup that you can make out of whatever material you want. Some people like more ornate metals like silver or pewter, while others prefer crystal glass or stainless steel. The chalice, which represents the element of Water, should be placed at the altar's western region.

The chalice is an important aspect of cake and ale rituals, and it occurs after several formal rituals. The liquid in the chalice represents the Earth's blood, and the cakes that accompany the drink represent the Earth's body, just like in the church ceremony. The liquid used varies per group and can be wine, fruit juice, or blessed water.

The Wand

This wand symbolizes the element Fire and should be placed at the South of the altar. Wands are a personal choice and traditionally should be around 50 centimeters or 21 inches. They should be made from wood that has been cut from a living tree and should be narrow at one point and rubbed smooth for an aesthetic and safe tool.

The wand can also be used like the athame to create visual effects and direct energy in various rites like love and prosperity. It works well for casting and uncasting circles and directing healing energies to those who need them.

The Pentagram Symbols

Let's start by dispelling the common myth that pentagrams are symbols of demons and black magick. That is merely Hollywood folklore, and it is absolutely false. For centuries, Wiccans and other magical communities have used the pentagram. It is a five-pointed star, and its points represent Water, Fire, Earth, Air, and Spirit.

History had shown the importance of the pentagram as far back as Ancient Babylonian times when it was used as a lucky charm to ward off evil spirits. It is strongly associated with a ritual known as the Lesser Banishing Ritual of the Pentagram (LBRP) and has become the most recognized symbol of protection in modern magick. Banishing is an intimidating term, but it simply means cleansing your aura from harmful elements. Consider what you're doing when you put the garbage out - you are simply banishing it to the tip.

When you have the power of the pentagram at your fingertips, you will feel elevated, energized, and feel the true power of its protection.

Chapter 2: Understanding Magical Rituals

How is your state of mind at this moment? Put it another way, how are you physically at this moment? Did you find the second question easier to answer? Why do we not take as much care over our mental health as we do with our physical health? You need to have a healthy psyche to perform magick. Just like you need a healthy body to perform physical tasks, you must have a balanced mindset to achieve the best results possible.

Why do other people attack you mentally or emotionally? In a perfect world, there would be no psychic attacks, and we would all have a restful and peaceful mind and be able to perform rituals and spells with ease. However, this is not a perfect world, and at some point, you will be the victim of a psychic attack.

It could be a person in your social circle that is envious of you and is projecting negative energy into your life.

It could be an attacker who has chosen to live a dark life filled with negativity and has cast spells to attack people who have chosen a different path.

The attack could originate from someone fearful and unwittingly projecting negative energy that has come into your life. They don't do this maliciously, but it still affects your psyche.

The attack could have originated in the spiritual realm, where a malignant spirit has found a critical vulnerability in your aura. Anxiety, depression, unhealthy addictions, and toxic relationships can all contribute to these issues.

Recognizing when you are Experiencing Psychic Attacks

Luckily there are distinct symptoms that indicate when you are under attack, so you can begin to repel the negativity.

These signs include:

- **You Are Inundated by Negative Thoughts:** Have you ever thought that someone or something has taken control of your thoughts? Normally, you have a balanced view of life and can recognize that most situations have a negative and positive effect on you, but recently you can't stop dwelling on the negative thoughts? A forceful stream of negative thoughts is a sure sign you are under psychic attack from another source. If you can't see beyond the negativity, you'll become fatigued and frustrated with life, leading to severe depression.

- **Dreaming of Yourself as a Constant Victim:** When you sleep, you are at your most vulnerable. Your dreams will be invaded by harmful energy and will make you fearful. The scenarios may differ, but the feelings of helplessness will be the same. You may dream you are being chased through unfamiliar environments, or your dreams could manifest into violent fights. Whatever you dream, it will be so traumatic that it will damage the quality of your sleep, leaving you lethargic and worn out the next day.

- **Phobias:** When you are under psychic attack, you will experience unrealistic bouts of fear. The car you drive every day will suddenly appear unsafe, and you will be too afraid to drive it. You may become so terrified of what lies ahead that you refuse to leave the house. These feelings will be so intense that they will be unlike any other feelings you have ever experienced. Normally, phobias are triggered by incidents, but these irrational fears often come from nowhere.

- **Lack of Energy:** Have you ever had a conversation with someone who drains you, mentally and physically. These are energy vampires, and they are the most common form of unintentional psychic attackers. As they drain the energy from you, they become more animated and livelier. Once you break free from their clutches, you need to sleep to recover your vitality. Recognizing these types of personalities is the first step to avoiding them.

- **Headaches:** Severe headaches that come from nowhere are a classic sign of a psychic attack. Normally, we can identify what causes regular headaches and treat the symptoms, but psychic migraines are violently painful and untreatable.

- **Trance-Like Symptoms:** When you talk to someone and then fall into a mental stupor as they speak, you could be under attack from another form of energy vampire. The attacker may be skilled in using their voice to send you into a hypnotic state so they can drain your energy – or they may be unintentionally draining you by overpowering you mentally.

- **Consistent Bad Luck:** This sign is frequently neglected when it comes to psychic attacks, but it shouldn't be. Most of us have a mixed fortune, and we experience good and bad luck, but when the good luck runs out, it could signify that you're being attacked. This sign can be difficult to spot, but it's important to remember that bad luck isn't always due to fate. It could be a sign of an attack.

Lesser Banishing Ritual of the Pentagram

This ritual can be as simple or as complicated as you like. Most practitioners use a dagger or magick knife to perform the ritual, but you can use your index finger. Dressing in a ceremonial robe is also an option, but wearing cool cotton clothes that allow movement will work just as well.

The LBRP is part of a mystical tradition and should be performed to clear your area and yourself before performing magick works. The ritual can also be performed when you feel you are under attack from malevolent forces seeking to drain your positive energy.

The kabbalistic cross is a key part of the ritual and involves visualizing yourself as an all-encompassing being that rises above the physical boundaries of the Earth while remaining grounded and anchored to the ground.

How to Perform the LBRP

The First Part of the Ritual

Step One: Visualize yourself standing on the ground and growing. Break through the physical boundaries that tower above you by reaching out your arms. Rise until you are taller than the city in which you reside. Soar above the continents, which become smaller as you get closer to the skies and continue to soar. Look down at the seas and landmasses, and you'll notice that they've shrunk into small dots.

Now visualize yourself venturing into the astral plane, where you can watch the planets circle the sun. They are simply toy balls for you to observe because you are so gigantic and magnificent. Even though the Milky Way is nothing more than a speck of dust in your environment, your feet remain firmly planted on the earth and feel as solid as a mighty root. You should observe a dazzling white light emanating from the Divine source once you've reached your peak. Direct this bright white sphere into your psyche with your dagger or sacred knife pointed to your forehead. Repeat the mantra A-Ta as you feel the light pulsating into your head.

Step Two: Bring your dagger, knife, or finger slowly down your body until it rests over your groin. The light will follow and fill your body with purity and light. When your hand reaches your groin, mentally instruct the light to travel past that point until it reaches your extremities. As it reaches your feet, compel it to travel down to the Earth and infinity and beyond. Repeat the mantra MAL-KOOT as you feel the vibrations fill your body.

Step Three: Raise the arm that is directing the light to your right shoulder. Visualize the light running down your core; extend it from your heart region, down to your right arm, and out into the universe. Repeat the mantra VI-GDOO-RA as the light shoots from your fingers.

Step Four: Repeat the exercise on your left side, and as the light appears from your left arm and through your fingers, repeat the mantra VI-GDOO-LA.

Step Five: Bring your hands together to your chest and clasp them together as if you are in prayer mode. This point will now emanate a golden glow while the white light continues to flow. This is the Kabbalistic Cross, and you are depicted as the center of the universe with divine light shining through your very core. Hold this position to feel the strength of the light.

The Second Part of the Ritual - the Formulation of the Pentagram

Step One: Move your body in an Eastern direction and face outwards. Move your arm from the left hip to the top of your head, drawing a pentagram with your knife or chosen object. Then draw a line from your head to your right hip, up to your left shoulder, and back to your left hip. As you link the last two lines, the light should be a glowing blue flame.

Step Two: Raise your hands to the side of your face while taking deep breaths. Feel the energy flow through you, filling you with love and joy. Raise the dagger or knife to point directly into the center of your blue pentagram, then point to the glowing image with your other hand while clenching the rest of the fingers into a fist.

Step Three: Immerse yourself in the pentagram by stepping forward with your left foot. As you feel the energy flow through your core, thrust your hands into the center of the pentagram. Repeat the mantra YUD-HE-VAHV-HE as the vibrations increase.

Repeat the movement until you have faced every direction and immersed every part of your body. Repeat the mantra EH-YEH when facing West, AH-GLA when facing North, and AH-DO-NEY when facing South.

Step Four: Return to your original position and use the dagger to connect the four points with white light. Extend the line to include the fifth point of the pentagram and return to the middle of your space.

Step Five: Now, look around you at the brilliant white sphere you have created with its blazing blue pentagram at its center. All the points of the space have been blessed with the names of the ancients, and they are working with you to achieve perfect protection from harm.

The Third Part of the Ritual - The Evocation of the Archangels

Evoking archangels is part of the ritual for people who believe in the power of archangels and wish to ask for their help to protect them and their families.

Not all practitioners believe in their efficacy, and this is a personal decision you must make depending on your beliefs.

If you believe, then take the following steps to evoke your favorite archangels and enlist their help:

Step One: Stand tall and form a cross by extending your arms.

Step Two: Envision a figure on a distant hill wearing robes. There should be a gentle gust of wind coming from the figure and a peaceful feeling in your heart. Depending on the feeling you get from each individual, use your instinct to evoke your archangel by saying "*Come to me (insert name of an archangel)*" until you have summoned your archangel.

Step Three: Move your left foot out and imagine a beautiful blue pentagram surrounding you. Say, "Around me flames the blessed pentagram."

Step Four: Visualize a golden star of Bethlehem around your heart and say, "Within me shines the power of the golden six-sided star"

The ritual is now complete, but some practitioners prefer to repeat the Kabalistic Cross to close.

Remember to keep notes about your rituals and what you encounter or feel in a ritual diary. This practice is the perfect way of noting what rituals work better under certain circumstances. Was the moon full, or was it waning? Did you perform your ritual outside or indoors? To create the ideal circumstances for the future, adopt a marking system and keep notes about how you felt before, during, and after your rituals.

The Middle Pillar Ritual

This ritual is based on the middle pillar of the tree of life featured in the teachings of Kabbalah. It represents the central point between the opposing pillars of severity and mercy. It cleanses the energy channels and allows the practitioner to channel external energy more successfully. Use it as part of your daily regimen to bring serenity and calm to your work.

Step One: Take deep breaths until you are calm and comfortable while standing in your work area. Turn your head to the East and relax your arms so that your hands fall naturally by your side. As you continue to take deep breaths, close your eyes and try to clear your mind.

Step Two: Raise your eyes so you are focusing on the space above your head. Picture a bright white orb similar to the light you visualized in LBRP and accept that this is the powerful force of the universe that has been dispatched to link you with the Divine energy. As the light grows and gets brighter, chant the name EY-HEYEY four times.

Step Three: Now, picture a powerful narrow beam emanating from the light that pierces the top of your head and enters you stopping at the base of your neck. This beam is your connection to your higher self and is a power that helps you discover what you are capable of. When the beam stops, imagine a smaller sphere of light at the end of it. Focus on the connection between the smaller ball of light and the ball that sits above your head. As you focus, chant the name YUD-HEY-VARV-HEY-ELO-HEEM four times.

Step Four: Concentrate on the ball of light in your neck and picture a beam emerging and traveling to your abdomen. Again, form a separate ball of light in this area and focus on the connecting beam while chanting YUD-HEY-VARV-HEY-ELOA-VIDAHAT four times.

Step Five: From the ball of light in your abdomen, visualize a beam that travels to your groin and forms another ball in your reproductive self. This ball represents your physical being, and as it grows and moves to fill the area, chant SHA-DIE-ELCHI four times.

Step Six: From this ball, visualize a beam that travels down to your feet, through your soles, and into the ground. The final sphere will appear partly submerged in the ground and partly above ground. This last link completes the connection to the ball above your head and finalizes the ritual. As you let your mind travel between the spheres, chant the name AR-DO-NY-HAAR-ETZ four times.

You will now have five separate spheres linked by brilliant beams of life that are channeling the energy of the Universe through your body. Remain in this scenario for as long as you like. Take deep breaths and feel the power of the Divine spirit flow through you until you are ready to end the ritual. Allow the images to fade and return to your regular life, knowing that the spheres and beams are still there even if you can't see them.

Kabbalah

There are a lot of misconceptions surrounding Kabbalah and why it is so important, but for our purposes, it is a concept that helps us understand the concept of the tree of life and why the individual sephiroth or spheres appear are key parts of protection rituals.

The tree of life comprises three pillars: severity, mercy, and a middle pillar representing balance or equilibrium. What is remarkable about its composition is how it relates to and functions in our central nervous system. We have the right and left hemispheres that act independently. The spinal cord runs through the center, distributing specific impulses throughout the body and maintaining a healthy balance.

The signals would cause chaos within the body if the central core did not manage them. We would become uncoordinated and directed by purely logical impulses if only the left side of the brain guided us. We wouldn't function properly if we didn't have the corresponding impulses from the right side of the brain that govern imagination. To put it in perspective, we would become highly skilled account managers capable of producing accurate numbers, but we wouldn't know what to do with them. We need the imaginative side of the brain to generate ideas to complement the logical conclusions provided by the left side of the brain.

This description is a simplified version of Kabbalah, but it illustrates why the tree of life is so important in this ritual. Understanding why you perform the rituals is just as vital as knowing how to perform them.

Chapter 3: Earth: Discover Your Power

Now that we can perform rituals that protect our whole selves, it is time to be more selective about the rituals and spells associated with the elements. The four elements are at the core of Western magick, and they have their origins in ancient pagan practices such as Wicca.

Elementals are the element's physical manifestation and have their origins in nature. This belief dates back to the Medieval Ages and has made its way into modern practices. Casting a circle involves enlisting the help of the four elements for protection and energy. The four cardinal directions are normally invoked in the following order: air to the east, fire to the south, water to the west, and earth to the north. These "corners "of the circle are guarded by watchtowers, which house the elementals representing the individual elements. A fifth element, spirit, connects the four elements and forms the pentagram's five-pointed star.

We will discover which elementals are associated with each element and what powers they have in subsequent chapters. This chapter is all about the element earth, so we begin with the corresponding elemental, which is gnomes.

Gnomes Are the Elemental Guardians of the Watchtower of the North

The word "gnome" originates from the Greek word "genomus," which means *earth dweller*. The spirit world of the element Earth is populated by gnomes who are traditionally hoarders and protectors of secrets. They are good-natured creatures who can easily interact with the physical world. They are presided over by the King of the Gnomes, Gob, who governs their land of hidden caves and underground dwellings.

They are mischievous and will often attach themselves to households with children with whom they feel a kinship. They can be seen by mortals and usually appear as small, wizened males and females dressed in blue or green outfits topped with jaunty red headwear. They are the guardians of the forest and gardens, and they protect all the wildlife and fauna there, which is why we traditionally have gnome ornaments in our gardens.

Just like there are many types of humans, there are many types of gnomes who have evolved through the ethereal body of the earth. You can call on them to help you with the magick associated with the element earth, including the following:

- Artistic endeavors
- Creating life balance
- Courtship and dating
- Learning to dance
- Creating harmony
- Seeking friendship
- Herbal spells
- Creating good luck
- Prosperity
- Romance, marriage, and seeking a soulmate
- Healing
- Becoming more social

Gnomes are attracted to everything organic, and one of the key ways to attract their attention is to fill your garden with plants and flowers. They love nature and will be helpful to anyone who takes care of nature. Even if you don't have a garden, you can invoke the gnomes by taking care of your indoor plants and buying organic food. Leave a tasty organic apple as an offering to entice the gnomes to join you.

Elemental beings are great companions and can be summoned with a well-kept garden, a crystal-clear water feature, or a roaring fireplace. Anything that represents the respect you have for their elements will attract these beings of light and pure energy. They will help anybody who is concerned for the environment and is seeking to improve their surroundings.

How to Invoke Gnomes

Some believers associate symbols and colors to the different elementals, and the one for the earth is a yellow square. The origin of these symbols is the Tattwa cards used in early Hindu philosophy to identify the basic elements.

When using the image to get in touch with elementals, you must take yourself to a quiet shady spot, preferably in a forest or woods, and sit directly on the ground. Take a small dish of soil with you and a picture of a yellow square. Begin the ritual by drawing the pentagram symbol in the air and concentrating on the Northern point to indicate your preference.

Now, concentrate on the Tattwa card with the yellow square and scatter your soil in a circle. Feel your conscious self move into the image and look for a portal to pass through. It should resemble a TV or cinema screen that you can pass through to enter a land of rolling hills and underground caves. If you successfully enter the kingdom, you should be greeted by a succession of gnomes who will welcome you with songs and dancing.

There are several types of gnomes, including:

The Forest Gnome: Generally shy of men, they will keep themselves hidden and only come forward when they are sure you are a friend and not foe.

The Garden Gnome: Older than his other counterparts, he will engage you in melancholy tales of gnome history. He will live in well-established gardens and have a cozy home.

Dune Gnomes: Slightly bigger than their woodland counterparts, and they dress in a drab way. They don't wear colorful clothes, preferring to dress in more muted tones.

House Gnomes: The most knowledgeable of the gnomes, they will be able to speak to you in your language, and they have visited the earth many times. They will lead any groups who want to interact with you. House gnomes are the family where Kings are chosen.

Farm Gnomes: They resemble house gnomes but are less interactive. Their conservative ways don't mean they aren't friendly, just a bit more conservative than house gnomes.

Siberian Gnomes: These are not always part of the group. These types of gnomes are more associated with trolls and other negative elements.

They will embrace you and bestow upon you their most treasured possessions. If they give you rocks and precious stones, it means you will be prosperous, while the gift of minerals means you will be blessed with a healthy relationship. Gifts from the world of nature should be treasured and respected. As the image of the world starts to fade, step back and return to the forest or woods where you began your journey.

Now you have a connection with these ingenious and capricious beings, and you should make sure you keep it healthy and thriving. Bring them offerings like fresh fruit and flowers or a vegetarian meal of nuts and berries regularly and say a thank you to them before you go to bed. Gnomes are great friends to have, but they can be troublesome if you don't respect their beliefs. Be mindful of nature and your relationship will prosper and flourish. Be disrespectful, and they will make their anger known; you will find your house in disarray and be plagued by bad luck.

Grounding and Centering Your Earth element

The earth element is the core symbol of balance. It represents the maturity of spirit, a point of balance between youth and old age. No matter your physical age, the earth element can help you discover the middle ground for life. It also has a powerful effect on the center of your body and organically connects with your organs to help your digestion and nourishment processes. When you connect and ground your earth element, you improve the functions of your stomach and spleen.

Grounding Exercise for the Earth Element

Imagine yourself as a mighty oak with deep roots and strong branches. Separate your legs and stand tall. Feel the ground beneath your feet and imagine your feet and legs as binding elements - they are the roots that stabilize you and make you feel strong.

As your roots delve into the earth, celebrate your security by spreading your arms as if they were branches of your tree. Imagine the haven they provide for wildlife and birds. Lift your face to the sky and feel the sun make your tree grow and flourish.

Stabilize your core with a relaxation response to aid your digestive system and improve your stomach health. Take a deep breath while relaxing your diaphragm and stomach muscles. The air will fill your lungs from the bottom to the top, making your stomach and thorax expand naturally. This form of stretching improves your muscular control and tones your core. Focus on your abdomen as you breathe, and pay attention to what happens when you inhale and exhale.

Center your body by creating essential oils to use on your body to address emotional imbalances like worry and anxiety and to create positive emotional triggers like empathy and love.

The earth element is represented by smells and odors that provide calm and resting qualities. They are designed to reassure you and put your mind at ease with their warm and earthy scents.

Essential Oil Recipes to Center the Earth Element

First, choose a carrier oil that will complement your oils.

- Sweet almond oil contains vitamins B1, 2, and 6 and vitamin E. It is a light clear oil that is easily absorbed and is perfect for dry skin. Don't use it if you have nut allergies.

- Apricot oil is perfect for older drying skin, and it is packed with vitamins and minerals.

- Jojoba oil is odorless and antibacterial. It can be used on sensitive skin and can help cure skin disorders like acne and eczema.

Essential Oils for the Earth Element

- Sandalwood

- Myrrh

- Fennel

- Coriander

- Cedarwood

- Ginger

- Rosemary

- Patchouli

- Vetiver

- Sweet Marjoram

Try this sensual, earthy mix to apply to pressure points on your body

- ½oz of almond oil

- ½oz jojoba oil

- 3 drops of sweet marjoram oil

- 3 drops of vetiver

- 3 drops of coriander

Blend for massaging or add sea salt to create a shower salt scrub. Apply onto pressure points to center your body.

- Acupressure point stomach 36 is located three fingers width below the flank of the leg. Stimulate on both legs for stomach harmony, a fortified spleen, and increased blood nourishment. It calms your nerves and promotes inner peace.

- Acupressure point Spleen 3 is located in the middle of the arch of the foot, in the depression on the side of the ball. It strengthens the spleen and resolves body temperature issues.

- Acupressure point Kidney 1 is located on the sole in the depression formed when you rest your feet on your heels. This is one of the best grounding points on the body. It removes negative energy from the top of the head to the upper body. When stimulated, it reduces anxiety and improves sleep. It stops hot flashes and agitation by centering and grounding the whole body.

Food that Feeds the Earth Element

Everybody knows the importance of diet when it comes to physical health, but the foods we eat can also help us balance our elemental selves. The earth element rules the body and is responsible for the digestive system without which we would all perish. Feed yourself the right foods, and you will be feeding the essential earth element as well.

Include in your diet:

- Root vegetables like onions, sweet potato, carrots, turnips, beets, and garlic. Any edible plant that grows underground is classed as root vegetables and is a tasty way to enhance your diet.

- Leafy greens like kale, collards, spinach, cabbage, and watercress are all packed with vitamins and provide a low-calorie ingredient that is filling and tasty.

- Light proteins like eggs, chicken, almonds, oats, yogurt, cheese, milk, and lentils are all important sources of protein that help you feed the building blocks of your most important organs like muscles and skin. The protein helps your body build and repair.

- Healthy fish like wild salmon, tuna, mackerel, cod, and sardines are filled with omega 3, which is great for heart health.

- Sweets that are natural like honey and fruit will help you avoid artificial sweeteners, leading to increased anxiety and an imbalance in your earth element.

A balanced earth element will support your freedom of expression and give you the confidence to reach your full potential. It clears the way for you to reach out to your spiritual self and ask for guidance. You will prosper and appreciate the world you live in due to your connection with the gnomes. You will have a strong sense of self-worth and the confidence to challenge those who try to bring you down.

Banishing Negativity from Your Earth Element

If you have an imbalanced earth element, you feel like you have no worth, and people don't listen to you. Your self-confidence will be in ruins, and you will be plagued with doubt. You feel disconnected and alone. Problems with your stomach and digestion will be among your health issues. Healing your earth element is just as important as healing any other wound or illness.

The earth element or the Muladhara in the chakra system is a stable part of your being. It should be as strong as a rock and give you the confidence to take measured risks and enjoy a sense of adventure. Suppose you are stuck in a rut or have trouble maintaining key elements of your life like jobs and relationships. In that case, it is time to work on balancing your earth element.

1) Get outside and commune with nature: Take your shoes off and let your feet feel the grass beneath it, or take a stroll in a bubbling stream. Leave all your electronics at home and fully immerse yourself in nature. Feel your stresses and woes float away as you let the wonder of nature calm your soul.

2) Color healing: The colors we surround ourselves with can influence how we feel. Earth tones like moss green and dark red represent the earth chakra, so try

adding these elements to your home and surroundings. Choose accessories made from natural materials and remove any plastic or artificial materials. Use a natural wool blanket to snuggle in and connect with the magic of a natural product to keep you warm.

3) Create herbal teas and infusions instead of your normal coffee and tea. Dried herbs and teas make a tasty, healthy alternative to caffeine.

4) Use salt to clean your sacred space. If you have an altar or sacred spot, cleanse it with a natural salt solution to refresh it and remove any harmful elements. When your space is cleansed, it will affect how your rituals work.

5) Place healing crystals around your home. Crystals are a powerful way to cleanse your aura, and you should keep them close when you feel ungrounded.

Earth Healing Crystals

Brown aragonite is one of the most effective crystals for the earth element. It unblocks ley lines and heals geopathic stress.

Black tourmaline eases tension in over polluted areas and can help clear interpersonal conflict.

Citrine links the heat of the sun to the center of the earth. It attracts energy and revitalizes the soul.

Spirit quartzes are available in many forms, and they can be used to stabilize the earth's energy while releasing harmful toxins.

Kabamba Jasper is a crystal formed from some of the oldest lifeforms on earth. It has a heart filled with ancient knowledge and will help you connect to the green kingdom to instruct you how to heal the planet.

Malachite absorbs radiation and pollution. This leaves the earth element cleansed and pure.

Rose Quartz is a peaceful, harmonious crystal that resonates with the guardians who watch over the earth. It is used to help people who have been involved in natural disasters and helps them regain their trust in earth's power.

Smokey Quartz absorbs negative energies and promotes healing.

Chapter 4: Air: Embrace Your Knowledge

Air is vital to the existence of humanity. It has an active quality and is associated with motion and movement. In magical terms, it represents the power of the mind, intellect, and imagination. It provides us with inspiration and knowledge and the strength and speed with which we can recognize truth and dispel lies. Air is a light active element that complements the dark and solid qualities of the earth element.

The element of air has many associations and is the element connected to the East. When the sun rises every day from the East, it signifies a place of new beginnings and new experiences. Using air elements in your magick will help you with the following:

- Creating a fresh start
- Attracting new love into your life
- Good luck with the lottery
- Making a fresh start with an ex-partner
- Changing career
- Creating a new business
- Any positive new ideas you may have

The elementals associated with air are described as sylphs, and they represent the connection to airborne things like birds, butterflies, and flying insects. They are also associated with griffins and Valkyries, and they rule the world of the Fae, where they sought shelter when the Celts banished the Sidhe race to the underworld.

They are described as air faeries who are shapeshifting tall humanoid beings with wings that span twice the length of their bodies, enabling them to swoop and soar through the skies like eagles. Their flights are impressive, and they create magical patterns in the sky with their wings, changing clouds into amazing murals just because they can. They aren't really interested in terrestrial matters as they are more concerned with the aerial world.

Sylphs are concerned about the increasing growth of air pollution and the poor health of the skies. They can clear the pollution left behind by airplanes and jets, and they can change the weather with their impressive wings. Sightings are rare because they are made of air, but they do make their presence known by swirling clouds that appear to have been brushed by feathers or an unexpected gust of wind. A sylph may have contacted you if you experience a swirl of warm wind on an otherwise cold day.

Although they rarely show themselves to humans, there is a symbiotic connection. After all, we breathe air, which is what they are made of. They also recognize that they need our help to heal the skies and lessen the pollution that threatens them, so these super-powerful beings seek to connect with people who have strong interests in the skies, weather patterns, birds, and nature. They will connect with a swirling breeze or a wind that seems to speak directly into your ear that makes you feel energized and strangely alive. When a sylph contacts you, it can lead to a startling moment of clarity and a fluttering sensation in your chest. Rejoice, a sylph has smiled on you, and that is a true blessing.

How to Connect to Sylphs

The Tattwa card associated with air is a blue circle, so print out the image on paper or visualize it in your mind. Choose a place where there is a body of calm water surrounded by a verdant green area for you to sit. Make yourself comfortable on the ground and close your eyes. Breathe deeply and chant the name of your favorite deity associated with air.

Deities Associated with Air

- Amun, the Ancient Egyptian god, depicted with the head of a ram or a snake

- Anemoi, the Greek Gods, associated with the wind who ruled the seasons and weather

- Fei Lian, the mystical Chinese creature who was as swift as the wind

- Paka'a, the Hawaiian god of the wind

- Ukko, the Finnish god of the sky

Slightly open your eyes as you ask the sylphs to visit you. Visualize the most beautiful birds and butterflies coming to land on you as you wait for your visitation. Relax and feel every breath of air on your face. You should feel a change in the air as you invoke these elusive spirits, and you may see them appear above the water. Watch as the light captures the flickering images that appear as darting grays and white flashes of energy. Sylphs love to show their agility and perform elaborate displays of their graciousness as they dart forward to tempt you and then retreat as quickly as light itself.

When you invoke sylphs, they will help to guide and inspire you to higher levels, especially in creative matters. They love to work with people who are natural movers and love to dance and create movement. Sylphs will help you heal your creative self and become the vessel for new ideas and innovative projects. Ask for their help to move forward from stagnant situations and discover your path in life.

How to Recognize the Need for Grounding Your Air Element

When your air element is unbalanced, you will notice the following symptoms:

- Your busy mind makes it hard to sleep

- Your ideas seem to be floating about and never come to fruition

- You can't organize your thoughts, they fly off in tandem, and you can't get them back

- Your breathing is erratic; you are out of breath without any reason
- Simple tasks leave you exhausted
- Your energy is dissipated by any form of communication, even emailing and texting
- There is too much static energy in your life
- You feel apathetic about your life
- There seems to be no point in life

How to Ground Your Air Element

Breathing Exercise for Grounding

1) As you wake in the morning, sit up and throw out your arms to embrace the day. Take a deep breath through your nose and release it through your mouth. Feel the pleasure of filling your lungs as you concentrate on refreshing your body.

2) Now, hold your breath for thirty seconds. Feel the vitality it gives you and the life-giving properties from this invisible element. Allow yourself just *to be* as the air leaves your body as you exhale.

3) Set your intentions for the day. Remember, every morning is a new start, so be sure to give voice to what you want from that particular day. "Today is going to be happy and full of joy. I welcome every experience and embrace life fully," say this before you rise and prepare yourself to face the day.

How to Ground Your Air Element and Bring Air Balance to Your Life

- Don't skip meals. Food is important, and taking the time to savor your meals will help you balance leisure and work times.
- Reduce stimulants like caffeine and alcohol; you shouldn't need them. Make the most of your natural thoughts and feelings.

- Cut back on your online presence. Turn off your phone and laptop and just pay attention to what's going on around you. Engage in conversations and ask real people for information the old-fashioned way.
- Chill out before you go to sleep, turn off the TV and read or take a long relaxing bath before you go to bed
- Censor what you see. Avoid vivid images of disasters and anxiety-inducing news stories. Concentrate on what is positive and uplifting instead.
- Burn off your nervous energy by exercising or taking a bike ride
- Lie on your back in a field and watch the clouds. Connect with the sylphs and watch their amazing patterns form in the sky
- Tend to your garden, plant flowers that attract bees and butterflies like helenium, aster, and echinacea
- Visit a butterfly house
- Fly a kite
- Join a birdwatching group
- Travel to high perches and watch the sun disappear over the horizon
- Use candles around the home and experience the satisfaction of blowing them out
- Start a new project like learning a new language or taking an art class
- Bring wind chimes into your home and garden

Synesthesia and Air Element

The ability to connect scents and secondary cognitive experiences is known as synesthesia. For synesthetes, the air is a vital element because it carries scents. Practice with various scents to see what happens. Colors, forms, and shapes will be experienced by some, while others will experience musical tones. It is normal for certain smells to bring back memories. For example, the smell of freshly cut grass may remind you of your father mowing the lawn, while the smell of the sea may bring back memories from vacations. Synesthesia is unique in that the scents evoke abstract associations and images.

You can take formal tests to determine if you are a true synesthete, but if you experiment at home, you can still get results. The scents most associated with the air element are peppermint, lemongrass, lavender, pink pepper, neroli oil, white musk, and orange flower. Use essential oils and candles to fill your home with these evocative scents and see what reaction they trigger. Even if you don't get random images or sounds, at least your home will smell amazing.

Casting a Magical Circle

Air is strongly connected to the dagger and wand, the magical tools considered essential for casting a successful circle to perform your work in. All four elements are equal in a magical circle, but the air has the casting vote because of its connection to the tools.

Step 1: Find a flat open space where you won't be disturbed.

Make appropriate representations for each element in the cardinal directions. A potted plant or ceramic bowl in the North represents Earth, a white feather or sprig of sage in the East represents Air, a candle or tea light in the South represents Fire, and a seashell represents Water in the West.

Step 2: Begin the casting

Face the East and relax. Raise your wand or dagger and envision the wind whipping around you and the air ruffling your hair. Say, *"Spirits of the Air, I call upon you to join this circle."*

Turn to face the South and picture flames surrounding you. Feel the heat on your skin and the power of the crackling flames as you say, *"Spirits of Fire, I call on you to join this circle."*

Turn to the West and feel the cold water flow around your body. The power of waves and currents force your body to sway as you say, *"Spirits of Water, I call upon you to join this circle."*

Finally, turn to the North and let the earthy scents and the feel of soil beneath your feet fill your senses. Breathe in the mossy tones and say, "Spirits of the Earth, I call on you to join this circle."

Step 3: Ground yourself

Imagine your feet growing roots that travel through the soil to connect you to mother earth and cement your strength. Now turn your face to the skies and say, *"Father Sky, I implore you to fill me with your strength,"* and welcome the golden rays of the Cosmos as they fill you with infinite power.

Step 4: Do your magick

Perform your ritual or spells knowing you are safe in your circle. The elements are looking out for you, and the Cosmos has your back.

Step 5: Close your magick circle

Perform the closing ritual by turning to the individual elements and thanking them for their assistance. Bring them into your consciousness and show them how much you appreciate them. Once you have completed your thanks and as you leave the area to resume your normal life, say:

"The circle may be open, but it is never broken; the love I have for you all is forever in my heart and head. We may have parted for now, but we will meet again."

Protect Yourself and Your Home from Negative Air Elements

Smudging your home with sage will help to cleanse and protect it from harm. Once you have cleansed your home, place feathers and bells at the entrance and on windowsills while decorating your personal space with air plants like alder and mimosa. Place crystals around your home - blue calcite, citrine, and yellow jasper are all associated with the air element. Diamonds and opals are associated with the air element, so wearing them will boost your energies and protect you from negativity.

How Does the Hexagram Protect Us?

We have already discussed the properties of the pentagram and how it relates to the elements, so it is a normal progression to use the hexagram to increase our levels of protection. The unicursal hexagram is a symbol that can be drawn in one movement and is a six-sided star that dates to 1588 – when it was mentioned in a paper about mathematics and the part it plays in magick and philosophies. The six-sided star is commonly thought to represent God, while the five-sided pentagram is more connected with man.

Alastair Crowley incorporated a five-petaled rose within the hexagram to give it additional connections to the divine union between a man and God. The petals represent the pentacle and the femininity of the divine world, while the six points on the hexagram equate to God. When the two numbers are added together, the result is eleven points, the ultimate number of divine union and magick.

The hexagram has become one of the more popular ways of invoking elemental forces to banish negativity and harmful energies because it can be drawn in one motion.

The Symbolism of the Unicursal Hexagram

- It has six points, which represent the four elements plus the Sun and the Moon. This gives it the power to invoke the cosmos and all the planetary elements alongside the more standard elements.

- The hexagram represents two halves of a whole. It promotes the union of opposites like male and female energies or mortal and spiritual worlds. The symbol represents a coming together of divergent parties to form a stronger and more balanced being.

- The unicursal hexagram gives you the strength to free yourself from all that binds you and become more successful. It gives you self-confidence and the power to find your path and follow it.

The hexagram has been another victim of Hollywood folklore. While the hexagram is not a common pagan symbol, it has gained appeal through its association with Kabbalah. The similarity to the Star of David draws it to Judaism, yet the regular hexagram isn't limited to religious beliefs. Some people believe it is a hex symbol, but studies have shown that the positive aspects of the sign far outweigh any negative influences.

Wearing a unicursal hexagram in the form of a pendant or other jewelry will offer you protection, while some people prefer to have the symbol tattooed on them. The design can be enhanced with other symbols but is just as powerful when used in its original form.

Other Magick Symbols You Can Use

The ankh is a magick symbol that is Egyptian in origin and is a symbol of life. The rounded top represents the female energy, while the lower straighter portion is male. The ankh amulet is a powerful way to protect yourself from evil forces.

The witch's knot is a powerful female magick symbol that dispels the negativity originating from male sources. Draw it over your door to ward off evil spells and people.

The Celtic shield originates from Ireland, and it represents the eternal flow of protection and life. It can be worn to keep the wearer safe from harm and help them live longer.

The Mars sign will help you counter any magick used against you and is an aggressive sign and can be used to cast some powerful spells. Using the *harm no one* rule, it should only be used for protection.

The horned god is a symbol of a circle topped with a crescent moon. It protects the home and brings courage and strength to the wearer.

Chapter 5: Water: Establish Your Boundaries

Water magick is associated with the West, the moon, and the power of the natural sources of this magical liquid. Imagine being able to harness the strength of the oceans, the seas, the rivers, and the ponds to use in your magick. Now increase that power by adding the natural force of rain, hurricanes, and raging storms. Add waterfalls and tidal waves to the pot, and you are beginning to see the elemental maelstrom that water represents.

Water is nature's most powerful cleanser. It puts out fires and floods the Earth to make way for new growth as it cleanses and purifies the ground. It gives life to the Earth and makes it verdant. Using water to power your spells and rituals will help you connect to the deepest parts of yourself.

Water Elementals

Undines are the guardians of the West and the element of water. They are an invisible species that inhabit the waters of the Earth and live to love and honor humankind. They are emotional beings who enjoy serving and assisting us in our magical endeavors. Several groups of undines inhabit their watery world. Some live in waterfalls and are described as nymphs, while the sea is home to mermaids and sea maids who can often be seen riding dolphins and other sea creatures. Water nymphs will often take the name of the streams and lake where they live.

They are ruled by Neptune, the king of the sea but are primarily female. Undines can take on human form, and legend has it that they adopted families of fishermen and watched over them while their men went to sea. Many humans have been enticed by the call of the sea to seek out undines and join them in their watery world.

Celtic mythology tells of an ancient Ireland populated by a race of semi-divine creatures who could live on land and also exist in water. Modern Celts believe they can still be found in the native marshes and fens in that area.

Invoking the Undines

The Tattwa symbol for water is a silver crescent moon, so print out the symbol or picture it in your head. Visit a place where there is a natural source of water and concentrate on your crescent moon. Ask the undines for help to connect with the element and wait for them to respond. They will cause ripples in still water or may even cause a visible wave. Watch for a signal that they are aware of your presence, and then welcome them into your aura. Undines are natural clairvoyants and will send you messages about what you need to know. Ask questions and be open to their interactions, and you may even glimpse a sight of a watery figure rising from the lake or stream.

Taking a ritual bath is a perfect way to connect to the element of water. It is also a relaxing and refreshing process that will prepare you for your magick work. The main aim of the ritual bath is to cleanse, but it can be much more. Hoodoo practitioners believe strongly that the power of the bath is one of the most evocative ways of performing magick. They teach us how to use herbal infusions to create intentions and bathe in the waters to make these intentions bear fruit.

Simple Cleansing Bath

You must scrub your tub before taking any ritual bath. Ensure your bathtub is completely clean because any residue from previous baths will make the water stale and less cleansing. Now fill it with hot water and cast three tablespoons of Epsom salt or purified sea salt into the tub. State your intention clearly, "Creature of the water; I call upon you to purify me," as you cross your arms to make a cross over your bath. Before you step into the water, declare your intention to cleanse it of all maladies.

Charge your bath with the names of your favorite deity, preferably water-based. Aphrodite, Ganga, and Neptune will all help you charge your bath and make it filled with positive energy. Chant with your favorite mantra and light candles around your tub to enhance the cleansing process before you submerge yourself in the water. Reciting prayers or incantations will help you relax, but you don't have to be religious for a ritual bath to work.

If you are uncomfortable with prayers or other fixed text, then choose your own way of relaxing. It can be the lyrics from your favorite song or a popular poem you love. If you make your intentions clear, the spirits will hear you. You must remain in the bath until all of the water has been drained. As the water flows away, visualize your problems and negative energies going down the drain.

Step out of the bath and allow yourself to air dry. You don't want to wipe any magical energy away with a towel. Put on some clean, fresh clothes and let the excess water soak into them. To get the most out of the cleansing, wear these clothes for 24 hours.

Charge Your Bath with Herbs for the Added Intention

Adding herbs makes your bath more specific to your needs. Take a cotton bag and place your required herbs into it, draw it closed, and put it in the water twenty minutes before you bathe. Leave the herb bag in the water for the duration of your bath.

Prosperity: Add cinnamon, bay leaf, dill, clove, and basil to attract wealth and good fortune. Your chances of success will increase, and good luck will come your way.

Money: If monetary success is more important to you than general prosperity, you can perform an additional ritual to complement your prosperity bath. Scatter some disinfected coins of any denomination in your bathwater. Place a small pot of honey on the side of your bathtub. While relaxing in the water, coat each coin in honey and stick it onto your skin. Write a wish on a piece of paper and light a green candle. Burn the paper before you remove the honeyed coins from your body and place them in a jar. After getting dressed after your bath, take the jar of coins and store it in a dark and cool place.

Love: If you are seeking a partner or want to attract romance into your life, add some dried rose petals, cilantro, mint, rosemary, and jasmine to your herb bag and soak for twenty minutes.

Uncrossing: Curses, jinxes, and other negative spells can be removed with a simple uncrossing bath if you believe negative forces are targeting you. Add peppermint, hyssop, lemon balm, and clary sage to heal your mind and soul from negative attacks.

Health Issues: Most people are fully aware of the healing properties of mineral baths and spas; if you visit them regularly, you are familiar with the benefits they can have. Adding salt crystals, herbs, and essential oils to your bath is a simple way to recreate this healing process.

Healing Herbs and Their Benefits

- Basil can help with joint pain, infection and virus treatment, congestion relief, and nervous system stimulation

- Bay leaf will help with diabetes, cardiovascular issues, menstrual problems, and insomnia

- Chamomile relieves stress and tension, as well as loss of appetite and skin problems

- Clove herbs increase energy and improve blood circulation

- Dill can help with cholesterol, epilepsy, and depression

- Lavender is an anti-anxiety and anti-acne herb

- Lemongrass helps boost the immune system, kills bacteria, and relieves muscle pain

- Myrrh aids digestion, promotes healing, improves blood circulation, prevents infections, and relieves spasms

Oils and Their Benefits

- Orange blossom oil is an aphrodisiac, anti-inflammatory, acts as a diuretic, and aids Alzheimer's treatment
- Peppermint oil soothes the digestive system, eradicates halitosis, increases energy, and releases natural energy
- Rose oil is an aphrodisiac, an astringent, a laxative, and a blood purifier
- Sage oil helps to maintain hormonal balance, lower cholesterol, fight infections, and repair the liver
- Thyme oil aids circulation, acts as an expectorant, detoxifies the body, and is beneficial to the heart

The Rose Cross Ritual

This ritual is meant to dampen astral flares and protect the practitioner from psychic attacks. It can be used to calm the mind and soul before sleep and is popular because of its simplicity and effectiveness. Some witches and practitioners shun the religious symbolism of the cross, but this is a common misconception. Even non-Christians can benefit from the symbolism of the cross as it is a powerful representation of the four elements. When you combine it with the circle, you get an all-encompassing symbol that any doctrine can use.

When you perform this ritual, you create a veil to mask your presence from any harmful influences. The pentagram and hexagram rituals light astral flames that make you visible, while the Rose Cross Ritual masks those flames.

Beginners should physically create the ritual to acquaint themselves with the workings and how they progress. When you become familiar with the practice, you can visualize the process as you lay back and relax. Lose yourself in the imaginary world as you get the sensation of performing the physical ritual in your head. Relaxation helps you release any pain or negativity as you bathe in the white light of Divinity that makes your mind ready for sleep.

The ritual can also be performed for other people. As you create the protective series of crosses, picture the person standing in the center of your area. Call down the light to shine on them as well as yourself. As the ceremony finishes, dispel the astral image and return it to the ether to ensure they are safe and benefit from the ritual.

How to Perform the Rose Cross Ritual

The ritual should be performed in a square space that has specifically placed corners. The symbols can be drawn with a stick of incense or an invoking wind depending on your preference.

Step One: Walk to the Southeast corner and make the symbol of the rose cross, a traditional cross with a circle that encompasses the point where the two lines meet and form the cross. The circle represents the rose and should stay within the bounds of the cross. Chant the name YEH-HEH-SHOO-A and vibrate the last syllable.

Step Two: Trace a line from the center of the rose cross to the Southwest corner and recreate the symbol. Chant the name YE-SH-VE and vibrate the last syllable.

Step Three: Trace a line from the center of your rose cross to the Northwest corner and recreate the symbol. Chant YE-SH-VE once more.

Step Four: Trace the line from the Northwest corner to the Northeast corner, recreate the symbol, and then chant.

Step Five: Finalize the pattern by making a line from the Northeast corner to the Southeast corner and repeat the chant.

Step Six: Trace a line to the center of your space from the Southeast corner. Recreate the cross symbol.

Step Seven: Join all the corners with a circle of intention to seal the independent crosses before returning to the center.

Step Eight: Trace another rose cross as large as you can and chant the name YEH-HO-VA-SHA as you unite the Tree of life with the rose crosses you have created. The sphere is now a solar protective vessel that will shield you from harm and keep you safe as you perform your magick.

The symbolism and the energies in this ritual are a powerful way to protect yourself, and you can customize it to meet your specific needs. Use the names of your favorite deities or angels to embellish the rose crosses. To emphasize your needs and requests, use colors and vibrations. The rose cross symbol can be used whenever you feel threatened or at risk. Trace it near the entrance to your house to protect both your home and you.

Consecrate Your Chalice

Your chalice is an important tool for water element magick because it holds water, so choosing the right one is essential. You can purchase unique and custom-built vessels online, or you can go with a more basic chalice for your work. Wooden, glass, crystal, and metal goblets work well, but you may prefer a more modern material. What matters most is that your chalice speaks to you, it is your embodiment, and it is treasured. Your chalice shouldn't be shared with others because that lessens its power. Consecrating your chalice makes it one of the most powerful tools in your magical arsenal.

You will need incense sticks, candles, sea salt, and water.

To represent your chalice's feminine or masculine aura, use the names Lady, Lord, God, or Goddess. Personalize it with your favorite deities, such as Thor and Freya, or go with a generic ceremony if you prefer.

Step One: Summon the spirits of the element water. These include serpents, sylphs, Osiris, Anuket, Damona, Selkie, Leviathan, or Olokun. Ask them to oversee your consecration ceremony and light your incense stick.

Step Two: Pass your chalice three times through the smoke of your stick and say, *"Let the power of the air purify you."*

Step Three: Light the candle and pass the chalice three times through the flame and say, *"Let the power of fire purify you."*

Step Four: Sprinkle salt and water on your chalice and say, *"By the power of water and salt be thee purified."*

Now bless and consecrate your chalice with an incantation

Lady of the water, the guardian of Femininity, bless this chalice

Lord of the seas and lakes, guardian of masculinity, bless this chalice

As it is used, let it be part of thy service and humanity

Let no harm come to this vessel, and let it be free of malice.

Ensure this is a vessel that will bring goodwill and harmony to the people it serves. I dedicate this vessel to your sacred works, and I name it (insert name) in honor of your love.

I dedicate my work and the use of this chalice to the gods and goddesses who rule the Earth and the Divine world beyond our vision. I vow that I will never cause harm and that I will always follow the rules of peace and harmony. So may it be.

Magick Waters and How to Use Them

Water magick spells are simple to cast because water is everywhere. It cleanses, quenches, and invigorates us, and it is a vital element of the magick craft. Charging your water with natural forces will increase the power of your liquid and make it more versatile.

Moon Water

Depending on what phase the moon is in, your water will contain different qualities. You choose which herbs to use and when to charge your water because this is an organic process.

What you need:

- Your chalice
- Airtight bottle
- Water
- Your chosen herbs
- Salt

Place your ingredients in your chalice and add the water. Place it outside or on a windowsill where the moon will shine on it. Leave it overnight but make sure you rise before the sun has touched it. Bottle and label it before sunrise. You can strain the water, or you can leave the herbs in; it's your choice.

Add a couple of drops to your ritual bath or anoint your forehead with moon water to invite dreams and visions. Use it to wash your hair to make it grow, or wash your hands in moon water to make them more creative. The uses are endless.

Sun Water

Based on the same principle as moon water, it is prepared during daylight and should be prepared before the sun goes down.

Use it to charge your magical tools and cleanse your altar. The sun strengthens and energizes your water, transferring that energy to your work when you use it.

Snow Water

This magical liquid is obtained from melted snow, and it is pure and blessed with the properties of ice. Use it to calm angry situations or clean away negative vibrations. Snow water from the first fall of the year is especially powerful for protecting your spells. It has transformation properties because it has undergone its own metamorphosis.

Rose Water

Simmering rose petals in your water is the simplest way to make this magical potion. Use rose water to attract love and romance to your life and create harmony in your present relationship.

War Water

Hoodoo practitioners will recognize this magical spell. Place nails, moss, and water in a jar for two weeks and allow it to sit. The water will be red or muddy in color, and it should be kept in the jar until it is needed. When someone is causing you strife or bringing "war" to your life, use your War Water to keep them away.

Chapter 6: Become a Pillar of Strength

Fire is a fascinating element as it represents different things to different people. The ancient people relied on it to provide warmth, cook food, and keep them safe. Fire provided them with light when it was dark, so it fueled their passions and illuminated their minds. It has the qualities that keep us alive, but it also has properties that can fatally burn you if not controlled. Of course, the other elements can be deadly, but there is something visceral about the power of fire and the danger it contains. Fire represents the ultimate transformation and rebirth, and it teaches us to respect and revere nature and its all-encompassing forces.

Fire is a masculine element with the qualities of brightness, motion, and activity, and it is the only element that doesn't exist independently in a natural physical form on Earth. It only exists by consuming other elements, representing the transformation of elemental substances into ash, light, heat, and smoke.

When you work with fire, you need to control the destructive aspect and enhance the cleansing power. Think about how controlled fires burn away the undergrowth and clear the way for new growth. When you use fire in your magick, you heal old wounds and break bad habits. Use your spells for purification, sex, and healing illnesses and disease. Fire gives life and makes things fruitful as it consumes darkness and brings celestial illumination.

Connect with Fire by:

- **Starting a New Project:** The more creative, the better. Fire rules passion, creativity, and mental stimulus. When you create something, it immediately lights your passion and connects you directly to the element.

- **Use Alternative Lighting:** Any kind of light fueled by fire will help you connect successfully to the element. Candles, oil lamps, and tea lights are all safe ways of lighting your home without electricity.

- **Exercise:** Fire is directly related to cardiovascular motion, so get those heart muscles pumping. Working out, cycling, swimming, or even dancing will keep you fit and get the element of fire coursing through your body.

Fire Elementals

Fire elementals are spirits of nature that exist in different forms in some of the most dangerous places on Earth. They can be dragons that lurk beneath the ground or firedrakes and fire faeries that live in volcanos. Salamanders are the easiest elemental to work with, and they live within every flame that is ever lit. They are gentle creatures, slim lizard-like reptiles that resemble their physical cousins who live in marshland and other wet areas.

The salamanders love to awaken your spiritual senses so you can identify the forces that surround you by transmuting their fiery natural energy. When evoked, they help us to find our better selves and become energized to cope with inner turmoil and the challenges we face in life. Call upon them when you need courage, self-resolve, and willpower. They will give you a much-needed kick in the butt to get you motivated. They will assist you in strengthening your auric field so that you can see what is in front of you clearly and cut through the garbage.

Physically, they will strengthen your immune system and improve your blood circulation if it is weak. Invoking salamanders can help you detoxify your body and mind – while also increasing your metabolic rate.

Invoking Salamanders for Self-Improvement

Find a calm place where you won't be disturbed and light a red candle. Sit down on the floor or in a chair and begin your invocation.

- Turn your face to the candle and take a deep breath. Visualize the Tattwa symbol of a red triangle to invoke fire.

- Ask the fire to bless your intentions and guide your spirit.

- Feel yourself attuning to the flame, draw the heat into your soul and let it flow through you as you become one with the fire.

- Think about your spiritual detritus. Let go of all your spiritual negativity and emotions. Release them into the flame and watch as they turn to ash. All of those negative emotional relationships should be severed, and negative associations should be discarded.

- Every breath you take should be cleansing and purifying. Feel yourself transcending above your problems and worries and reaching a higher plane.

- Ask your salamander guide to make themselves known to you and open your senses to their presence. Feel them emerge from the flame and know that they are with you.

- Ask for their guidance about your health, life, relationships, and career. Be curious and ask them about themselves and why they chose to appear to you.

- The salamanders may have sensed a need in you of which you aren't aware.

- Once you have finished communications, thank the salamanders for their help and blow out your candles.

- Take a cool drink of water and relax as you contemplate the messages you have been given and the energy you now possess.

Consecrating Your Magick Tools

The elements earth and water are used to cleanse your environment, while air and fire consecrate the tool and make it more powerful and magical. Smudging your tools improves their effectiveness and makes them more ready for use.

Smudging with Sage

Choose a room that is well ventilated, and make sure you open all the doors and windows. Scatter salt around the base of your altar and sprinkle some moon water or blessed water to cleanse the area.

Lay the tools you want to consecrate on your altar. Take a bundle of sage and light it from a red candle. As the smoke builds, spread it to cover the tools. Say,

"Spirits of the fire, I ask for your blessing. Join us in sanctifying these magick tools to do good and bring joy to the world."

Remember to catch the ashes in a fireproof dish as your bundle burns.

Now, disperse the smoke with your arms or a broom. Stagnant energy will make our tools ineffective, so make sure you clear it all away. Bury the sage remains in the ground and store your tools in a cool and dry place to retain their strength.

Smokeless Method

If you prefer to work smoke-free, then try this simple consecration method instead.

You will need:

- A white candle
- Water
- Sea salt
- Incense

Cast a circle and light your candle and incense. Put the salt in a bowl and pass your chosen tool over the salt while saying, *"I consecrate this wand, my trusted fire tool, and charge it with your energies."*

Do this at all the four cardinal points of your space and call to the guardians who watch over them. As you complete the four points, stand in the center of the circle, and lift your tool to the skies. Say,

"I charge this tool with the power of the ancients, the solar deities, and the power of the moon." "I consecrate this tool and dedicate it to my workings, keep it charged and powerful so I can aid humanity and bring joy."

Fire Spells and Rituals

Sometimes specific people or situations can hold you back. They can't be dispelled with a simple cleanse because they are so entrenched in your psyche, they need stronger magick to get rid of them. Cord-cutting spells are designed to help you separate yourself from trauma so you can reevaluate with a clear head. When you cut cords with fire, they can be difficult to join again, so make sure you know what you are doing.

What you need:

- 10-inch black cord
- White or black candle
- Candlestick
- Images of yourself and the person or thing/place
- Paper and pen
- Matches
- Olive oil

Place your candle in the candlestick and dress it with the oil and any dried herbs you choose. Write the names of the people involved, including yourself, put the names and the pictures together and then tie them to opposing ends of the cord. Light the candle and visualize how your life will look without the negative element in it. Imagine your heart healed, happy, free from trauma, and filled with love and positivity.

Use the flame of the candle to burn through the cord and separate them completely. Breathe deeply and, with that breath, exhale any feelings of resentment or tension you still feel. Imagine them floating away and leaving your aura forever. As the candle burns down, meditate on your future and how you will progress from here. Use the melted wax to seal the picture and name of your nemesis before burying it in the ground.

You can adapt this spell to banish someone rather than just cutting the cord. Replace the white or black candle with a purple one, and it will cut the person or object from your life completely. A banishing spell should only be used as a last resort.

Attraction Spell

Not strictly protection magick, but we all feel safer when we are in a strong relationship or feel like part of a team. The element of fire is particularly effective when used in attraction spells, so now may be the right time to try one. Love spells are some of the most misunderstood spells in magick as you can't force someone to love you, but you can attract them to you. What happens after that is down to natural forces.

Attraction isn't always about love or romance. You could attract someone who will be a friend for life, or you may attract new opportunities. Be open to everything that comes your way, and you are sure to find happiness.

What you need:

- Two pieces of paper and a pen
- Fireproof vessel
- Matches
- Zest from an orange or orange essential oil
- Sealable bottle
- Wax

Set your intentions by writing the goal of your spell on the first piece of paper. Now, write the person it is intended to attract. The first statement works best if it is written as an "I want" statement that is concise. The second statement can be the name of a specific person or job you want or describe what you are looking for. Think of it as a Tinder profile for magick! Now, write your name on paper above the object of your desire connecting and binding you to them.

Place both strips of paper in a fireproof vessel and set them on fire. The ashes should be placed in a sealable jar, which should be sealed with wax. Place the jar on your altar until you have attracted what you desire. Break the seal and let the ashes blow away in the wind if your mind or desires change.

Unblocking Spell

Sometimes we are the only ones preventing our own progress. We become stuck in a circle due to doubt, frustration, or a lack of confidence. An unblocking spell clears the fog and allows us to progress to greater heights.

What you need:

- A white candle
- Cloves
- Peppermint oil

First, hold the candle and envision what you see as your greatest hurdles. What stops you from doing things? Doubt, fear, or lack of confidence are the usual suspects, so transfer them to the candle. Visualize them seeping into the wax and becoming part of the candle. As they enter, the candle will feel warm and bigger than it was before. Dress the candle with the oil and cloves, and then place it in a safe place. As you light it, feel these negative emotions and feelings dissipate with the smoke. Finish your ritual with a cleansing ritual bath and feel the confidence and strength return.

Perform the Lesser Ritual of the Hexagram (LRH) for Extra Protection

The Ritual

1) Stand up with both feet placed together. Your right arm should cross the front of your chest while your left arm falls to your side. Hold your preferred tool in your right hand with the apex upright.

2) Call upon your chosen deities, including Virgo, Sol, and Osiris, while chanting the magical formula of your choice. You can use the Hebrew words YO-NUN-RESH-YO, which relate to a solar elemental ritual or a Christian

alternative.

3) Extend your arms to form the sign of a cross and say, *"The sign of Osiris as he lay slain" or your alternative.*

4) Raise your right arm keeping your elbow square, and lower your left arm in the same way. Cast your glance over your left shoulder, so your eye line follows the left forearm and say, *"Isis is mourning."*

5) Now, move both your arms above your head, so they form a roof, and throw back your head as you say, *"Apophis and Typhon, this is your sign."*

6) Fold your arms across your chest and say, "Osiris has risen."

7) Repeat the third movement and say, "Oh, light of the cross" as you progress to movement 6.

8) Now, take your wand and create the sign of the hexagon of fire as you say, *"AR-AR-ETA."*

9) Retrace the upper apexes of the two equilateral triangles that form the hexagon.

10) Now, invert the hexagon symbol while repeating the chant *"AR-AR-ETA."*

11) Repeat while facing the East and the North.

12) When completed, each direction should contain an inverse and a reverse hexagram to protect the practitioner.

As the ritual is repeated and improved, the hexagrams will become more charged. Remember each pair of hexagrams represent elements, and they will radiate the power of each. Meditate and reflect on what you can gain from each symbol and become the embodiment of their joint powers.

The Advanced Middle Pillar Ritual

This ritual is an advanced way to clear blockages in your energy centers and channel positivity. This helps us connect to the Divine beings and communicate with higher astral planes. The Kabbalistic cross dictates how the ritual progresses and highlights the importance of the spheres it places at various parts of the body. Once you understand what the different points mean, you can personalize the ritual to concentrate on your needs.

The Ten Spheres of the Kabbalistic Cross

    1) Kether, meaning crown, sits at the top of the head

    2) Chokmah sits to the left of Kether and means wisdom

    3) Binah, at the right, means Understanding

    4) Chesed, at the left shoulder, means Mercy

    5) Geburah, at the right shoulder, means the severity

    6) Tiphareth, at the breastbone, means Beauty

    7) Netzach, at the left hip, means victory

    8) Hod, at the right hip, means splendor

    9) Yesod, at the groin, means foundation

    10) Malkuth, at the base of the feet, means kingdom

The practice imagines a bright spirit light traveling through and within the spheres to energize the subject. The light can be magnified by using the names of deities or spirits to fuel the power and increase the spiritual vibrations. You can create your own journey through your body and visualize a cornucopia of colors to compliment your vocal vibrations and vocalization. Personalize this ritual by cleansing your sacred space before you begin your journey to stay safe and keep your channeling healthy.

The names of the spheres can be used to intensify the experience, and the spirits of the elements will help you perform well. Use the ritual to create energy and harmony between your spheres, and you will fill yourself with positivity and peace.

Chapter 7: Staying Safe in the Astral Plane

Traveling the astral plane is one of the most exciting and satisfying things you can do, but some people don't experience it because they are afraid of what will happen. It may sound dangerous, but the truth is if you follow the rules and do it properly, you will be perfectly safe. Why would you deny yourself the experience if it can be done safely?

Astral projection is often referred to as an out-of-body experience or OBE. It is an interesting concept that is often associated with near-death experiences. While this can be true, we are more concerned with intentional travel when deciding if and when we leave our physical selves and travel beyond earthly boundaries. Astral travel allows you to explore the universe and beyond and discover the wonders that lie beyond your imagination.

Common Misconceptions about Astral Travel

1) You can be killed when having an OBE: Simply not true. You don't leave your physical body. You just detach yourself from it. You can only die when your physical self expires, so the only way this can happen is if your physical self dies while you have an OBE, then you die, period. It is worth noting that it is very unlikely for harm to come to your physical self when you are away from it. The natural alarm system will kick in, and you will return from your travels if your physical form is threatened.

2) Getting lost when traveling: Although the astral plane is vast beyond our comprehension, it is impossible to get lost there. When you travel through the ether, your soul never actually leaves your body. You make a copy of yourself when you experience an OBE and send it off to explore. This means your physical self is still capable of looking after itself and registering earthly happenings while your facsimile is free to discover the wonders that lie outside of our world.

Real Dangers of Astral Travel

Of course, there are risks in anything we do, but they can be avoided if we employ the appropriate protective measures. Knowing what can happen if we don't prepare is the best form of protection, so we'll start there.

1) **Possession:** When you travel, you won't be alone. Some of the entities you encounter will be malignant but remember; you have the power. When you perform magick on the Earthly plane, you know you can be subject to attacks from negative energies. Astral traveling is no different, but possession can only happen if you invite the entity in or are weak and have low protective vibrations. Providing you are firm with the spirits, they cannot invade your personal space.

2) **Sexual Temptations:** There's a good chance you'll be tempted to engage with entities who appear attractive and sexually appealing. These types of demons are known as succubus and incubus. They are alluring and know how to seduce you, but you must resist temptation. Sexual interactions can deplete your vitality, leaving you vulnerable and weak.

3) **Fatigue:** Although you may look asleep in the physical world, you are using up valuable energy when you have an OBE. This can impact your regular life and leave you tired and stressed. Don't sacrifice your rest for astral travel and only attempt it when your energy levels are high. You wouldn't travel in a car when exhausted, so don't perform astral travel when fatigued.

4) **Being You Out of Your Comfort Zone:** Astral travel isn't for novices. You should have experience in magical and spiritual practices and deep knowledge of what types of beings inhabit the realms. Thinking you will only encounter like-minded spirits is naive and dangerous. The astral plane is home to different forms of energy with a myriad of emotional responses. There are playful beings, and there are harmful spirits with many layers of intent separating them.

Beings of the Astral Plane

- **Celestials:** Angels, guardians, and spirit guides form the celestial class, and they are good-natured beings who only want to help and protect you.

- **Dragons:** While our conception of dragons is huge reptiles with sharp teeth and huge wings, the astral version is different. They can appear in any size or color and are recognizable by their fiery breath.

- **Demons:** Technically, there are demons on the astral plane because the definition of demons is a bad entity or spirit. They are interested in you because you project energy that they seek to possess. You will attract them if you enter the realm fearful, so leave your fears behind and simply stay strong. The astral plane is populated by mostly good-intentioned entities who will never try to harm you. The bad spirits won't harm you if you don't fear them.

- **Elementals:** As we have discovered, all elements have elementals, and you will find them just as prevalent on the astral plane as they are on earth. Say hi to the goblins, sylphs, salamanders, and undines as you pass them by.

- **Fiends:** Classified as beings made from negative energy, these chaotic individuals will cause you nothing but grief. Avoid them, and you will be fine.

- **Spirits:** The souls of those who have died on Earth wander the celestial planes. Don't be afraid of them; they are merely representations of their former selves.

1) **Becoming Overwhelmed:** Astral travel will be an eye-opener for you. You will see things so far from what you know that you can get freaked out and panic. Remember, you can return to the safety of your physical self whenever you like, so take comfort from that knowledge. Expect the unexpected, and you will be able to cope better. Nothing can prepare you for what is going to happen, so chill out, stay mentally strong and welcome the experience.

Another common mistake for beginners is to freeze when they reach the astral plane and stay in one position. Start with simple instructions and intentions and then build up to more complex routines. One of your first intentions could be "fly over my body and then return" or "travel to the top of my house and look at the roof." Goals that are simple and easy to achieve – but still awe-inspiring.

2) **Obsession:** Just like all the great things in life, you can become consumed by astral travel. Activities can reach an obsessive level and take over your regular life. Just like a video gamer can lose hours trying to escape from reality, astral travelers can become lost in their obsession. This isn't a real danger of astral travel. It is something that happens to the person who is practicing. Try and keep a balance between your two realities and remember that real life is more important. Astral travel should be a distraction

and a pleasure. If it develops into anything more, take a break and return at a later time.

Positive Affirmations in Astral Travel

We have already learned how important intentions and affirmations are when performing magick and spells. The same principles apply to astral travel, and you need to state your intentions strongly and back them up with positive affirmations to keep yourself focused and safe.

State your intentions to be successful and embrace the experience you are about to try. Do you want to revisit somewhere you have already been, or is it your intention to explore beyond your normal bounds? Only you know what you hope to achieve, so your intentions are a personal log of your thoughts, hopes, and dreams.

Affirmations are different. They are statements of belief, and they can be your own thoughts, or you can use messages that have originated from other people. We are bombarded with affirmations every day of our life although we don't always know it. Our parents encouraged us with words and phrases to convey what they wanted for us and how they hoped we would evolve. Friends, teachers, colleagues, and peers are just a few examples of people who will have provided you with affirmations and encouragement during your life.

These repeated messages are part of our subconscious and play a major role in how we evolve. They determine what sort of people we become and what we achieve. Without positive affirmations in our life, we would be more pessimistic and fail to achieve our goals.

When affirmations are paired with intent and action, they become even more powerful. They encourage personal growth and teach us to focus on our actions rather than trying to influence other people's behavior. This type of control helps us to gain self-confidence, inner strength, and compassion for others. These traits help you develop into a well-rounded individual prepared for anything and who knows how to achieve their wildest aspirations.

The best kinds of affirmations are written from the heart. They can be used to identify your negative, self-destructive thoughts and remove them. What is stopping you from progressing onto bigger and better things? Spot the negatives and use affirmations to counter the effect they are having on your life.

How to Write Positive Affirmations

- **Use a Language You Are Comfortable with**: Imagine yourself saying the phrase to others as you write. Affirmations should be concise, and elaborate verbiage will only serve to obfuscate their meaning. Make them succinct and to the point. Use words that lift your spirits and put you in a good mood.

- **Keep them in the Present Tense:** Affirmations are speaking to you at the moment. You can use dates to confirm when you want to achieve something, but your language should be set in the present, not the future or the past.

- **Use Positive Language:** Use "I am" or "I will" instead of "I won't" or "I am not" to keep your attitude positive. These instructions are meant to rally you, not criticisms of what you can or will not do.

- **Use Your Name to Personalize Them**: If you are comfortable talking about yourself in the third person, then go for it! It is not for everybody, but some people find that using their name strengthens and intensifies affirmations.

How to Use Your Affirmations

There are many ways to incorporate affirmations into your life, but these three will give you a good idea of just how simple they can be:

- **Repetition:** Set your affirmations to music so you can sing them in your head whenever you like. Repeat them to yourself several times a day to boost your self-worth and energy. Wake every morning and spend a minute saying them in your head. Whatever works for you, if your affirmations are repeated, you will benefit from them. Starting and ending your day with them will soon become a habit you grow to love.

- **Write Them on Your Belongings**: What do you have as your screen saver? A picture of your other half, a cute cat picture, or a random holiday snap? Change it to a positive affirmation or even a list of them to remind you how much you must look forward to in the future.

- **Add to Home Decoration:** Enter any home decoration store, and you will see examples of affirmations for the home. Artwork, picture frames, cushions, throws, bedding, and pottery. There is no end to examples of affirmations for the home. Although they were written by someone else, they can still serve as an inspiration for you.

- **Create an Inspiration Board**: Pick a space where you can see your board easily and then cover it in text, quotes, pictures, and affirmations that speak to your soul. Create a hotbed of spiritual strength that you can use whenever you need a boost.

Examples for Astral Travel Affirmations

- I am consciously choosing to travel on the astral plane
- I will embrace the experience and enjoy my journey
- I am much more than just my physical body
- I welcome the chance to travel beyond earthly boundaries
- As I sleep, I am completely aware of my activities, and I know how to keep myself safe
- I have the power to separate my physical body from my consciousness as I sleep

These affirmations will help you reduce fear levels and clarify what you expect to achieve. Visualizing your body as it rises and leaves your physical realm will help you make your affirmations stronger. Remember, you are the author of your own destiny, so you alone can make this endeavor a successful one.

Magical Amulets and Talismans

Amulets and talismans are used interchangeably by non-magick people, but those in the know are aware of the differences. Talismans are physical objects that are charged with magical energy to attract certain things to the wearer. They can be charged with intentions that represent health, wealth, job satisfaction, love, romance, or prosperity. Amulets are charged with intentions that are designed to protect the wearer from harm. They guard against psychic attacks, malignant spirits, and physical and spiritual accidents and have been used for thousands of years in many cultures.

They can be fashioned into any size or form depending on the demands of the person designing them. Some cultures displayed huge talismans and amulets in public places to demonstrate their beliefs and protect the community. Today, magical users prefer to create smaller, decorative objects that can be worn as part of their everyday outfits.

How to Create Magical Objects and Charge Them with Power

Step One: Define the objective of your charm

Be specific yet brief. Choose positive objectives that have been traditionally associated with talismans for generations.

Talisman Associations:

- Wealth
- Luck
- Prosperity
- Fame
- Success
- Love
- Romance
- Business success
- New career

- Job satisfaction
- Relationship success

Amulets Associations:

- Psychic protection
- Safety
- Creating a psychic shield
- Safe travel
- Protection for magical activities

The best way to remember what they represent is to take the initial letters - **A** for "amulet" to mean "away" and **T** for "talisman" to mean "toward."

Step Two: Choose the form

The form you choose should be both practical and aesthetically pleasing. If you are going to carry it around with you, it should be small and practical. Most forms chosen are coins, rings, pendants, necklaces, key fobs, bracelets, decorated cards, and material squares that have been decorated with the tapestry.

Make sure the object corresponds with your desire as much as possible. If you want to attract prosperity, use a coin or banknote to form your talisman. If you can't find a relevant object, you can use a blank metal disc or a piece of paper to inscribe your intentions.

Protective amulets can be made from anything, but some stones, crystals, and symbols are especially powerful. Use these ideas to give you some inspiration as to what to fashion your amulet from:

- Protective crystals and stones include jet, amethyst, hematite, malachite, black tourmaline, moonstone, labradorite fluorite, smoky quartz, amber, blue kyanite, and fire agate.

- Sigils and symbols include runes, the eye of Horus, Hamsa, Triquetra, Inanna's knot, and the scarab. Research the symbol or sigil that appeals to you aesthetically and spiritually, and incorporate it into your amulet.

- Totems and animal guardians, just like the elementals, can bring their physical powers to your aid to keep you safe in the spiritual and astral realm. Wolves, tigers, lions, eagles, bears, hawks, dogs, and cats all have individual qualities you can use in your amulet.

- Pictures of your favorite deity or relatives can be used to ask them to watch over you. Amulets containing mementos from departed loved ones can be both powerful and comforting.

Talismans can be worn simultaneously as amulets to provide you with a full range of protection and attraction. They don't cancel each other out, and their powers can complement each other. Your amulet will clear the path for your talisman to attract with a stronger pull.

Choose your talismans depending on your imagination and preferences:

- Stones and crystals to increase and draw intentions, including amethyst, rose quartz, iron pyrite, tiger eye, hematite, emerald, agates, tourmaline, shiva lingams, and carnelians. These stones and crystals will heal your body as they attract love, prosperity, and happiness to your life.

- Sigils and symbols including Kibera yantra, Lakshmi, Ganesh, the Fehu Rune, Oshun, and Maneki Neko represent the different religions and cultures that believe strongly in the law of attraction.

- Images of gods and goddesses will enhance your talisman and bring you different intentions for your individual needs. Aphrodite attracts love and passion, Cupid, Andrius, and Yebisu bring luck, and Ganesha and Freya represent fertility and abundance. Thor represents power, and Odin represents wisdom.

How to Charge Your Amulet or Talisman

- Once you have determined what your piece is, an amulet or talisman, it's time to charge it with corresponding energy. Cleanse the item with a sage smudge or by burying it in a bowl of salt for an hour so it is clean and ready for charging.

- Time your ritual to correspond to your intent. For instance, if you want to attract love or passion, charge your talisman at the next full moon. To ward off evil, choose the next waning moon.

- Hold the object in your hands and visualize what your intention is. For fifteen minutes, direct your energy and intent into the object and hold the visualization as long as you can.

- Now, leave them out overnight to soak up the moon's rays.

- When you pick your object up in the morning, remind yourself what the intentions are before you wear it.

Your sacred objects should be recharged monthly to keep enchantment levels high.

Chapter 8: How Grimoires Can Protect You

What Is a Grimoire?

The simple definition of grimoire is a magical book that contains spells, rituals, ingredients and their use, prayers, incantations, techniques for divination, and other magical information. They can be ancient books written by historically important figures, or books written by modern witches practicing today.

The name originates from the French language and is an old spelling of the word "grammaire" that we recognize as grammar in English. The dictionary defines a grimoire as a magician's handbook that can invoke the dead and demons. In reality, most grimoires are much more detailed than that, and you can choose how complicated and in-depth you want your knowledge to be.

Grimoires can be filled with information and contain hundreds of pages, or they can be short leaflets that relate to certain magical workings and practices. Before the invention of printing, press magick was shared by word of mouth or handwritten text that was passed from one person to the other. Some ancient grimoires survived through the ages and provided a fascinating insight into how witchcraft and magical practices evolved.

One of the key examples of a grimoire that is still considered relevant today is the Key of Solomon. It is still studied today and has become one of the most popular Middle Age grimoires ever. The Key of Solomon is divided into two books that deal with seals and pentacles associated with angels, demons, and other spirits and the connection to certain planets and solar energies.

The Key of Solomon

Book 1 contains the seals and pentacles of Solomon with instructions on how to use them. They can be used by the operator (also called the exorcist) to summon the spirits of the dead to compel them to do their will. The spells and incantations are used to find items that are lost, how to become invisible, seek success, and find love. The pentacles listed in the book all have certain relevance that leads them to different magical practices.

The Pentacles of Solomon

The Sun Pentacles have seven different designs that are associated with them:

1) The first pentacle contains the face of Shaddai the Almighty and the angel Metatron, who both have power over the creatures of the Earth, and you can use this pentacle to control animals and nature.

2) The second pentacle represents the pride and arrogance of those who oppose the user's wishes. Use it to silence people who want to dominate you.

3) The third pentacle of the sun is used to invoke the power of the twelve tribes of Israel.

4) The fourth pentacle gives the user the power to see others as they are. The spirits can discern even the most hidden parts of someone's mind and heart and reveal them to the operator.

5) The fifth pentacle enables the operator to travel long distances in a short time. It also gives the power of sight into the future or the past by providing visions in dream form.

6) The sixth pentacle offers the user the power of invisibility, allowing them to move among others without being seen.

7) The seventh pentacle frees the user from the bonds and locks that bind them.

The Moon Pentacles have six different designs that are associated with them:

1) The first pentacle has a hieroglyphical image of a gate and has the power to unlock any doors or gates that hold the user back. This first seal is the key to unlocking the power of all seals, granting the user access to all the powers resulting from the removal of all obstructions.

2) The second pentacle protects the user from all water-based perils and dangers. Natural phenomena like hurricanes, tsunamis, and tempests are all associated with the Moon, so this pentacle gives you the power to calm them and stop them from harming the user.

3) The third pentacle protects against attacks that happen at night and over water. They dispel the power of evil spirits who haunt the users' visions and dreams.

4) The fourth pentacle protects the user from all injuries to both the body and soul.

5) The fifth pentacle protects the operator from nightmares and helps them find the answer to their questions through their dreams.

6) The sixth pentacle is a powerful talisman to bring rain and water to people and places that need them.

The Mercury Pentacles have five different designs associated with them:

1) The first pentacle is used to invoke the spirits who dwell in the lower firmament and guard magick's deeper knowledge and workings. They have deep associations with elemental spirits and the guardians of nature.

2) The second pentacle has the power to fulfill wishes that are beyond the realm of possibility. It can also be used to protect expectant mothers and the fetus they carry.

3) The third pentacle invokes the spirits responsible for creativity and literary skills. It can aid writers, poets, and authors to improve their skills and impress others. It is also the pentacle associated with alchemists and can provide the operator with secrets and knowledge of hidden realms and how to cross into them.

4) The fourth pentacle can help the operator read other people's minds and penetrate their hidden thoughts. There is wisdom and virtue that lead to a piece of greater knowledge and perception within this pentacle.

5) The fifth pentacle opens all doors and removes obstacles. It allows the operator to lift their heads and greet the King of glory.

The Venus Pentacles have five different designs associated with them:

1) The first pentacle is governed by the angels of Venus, who will diminish the power of false prophets and dispel their thoughts and influences. They also work with the operator to manifest their desires and hopes.

2) The second pentacle empowers the operator with love and passion. It attracts all manner of grace and honor and inspires the operator to live a righteous and honorable life filled with love and respect.

3) The third pentacle attracts respect and love to the operator. It empowers them to reproduce and replenish the earth with love and admiration.

4) The fourth pentacle is used to inspire lust and desire towards the operator. It has the power to entice and enchant others and draw them to the operator. It also gives the knowledge of how to dispel such enchantments when the time is right.

5) The fifth pentacle draws people into the user's social circle. It makes the operator inexplicably attractive to others, and they are like moths to a flame.

The **Mars Pentacles** have seven different designs that are associated with them:

1) The first pentacle helps gain courage and strength ready for battle. It serves all manner of warriors to be filled with enthusiasm and overcome all physical barriers to become accomplished combatants in all fields of endeavor.

2) The second pentacle holds power to fight diseases and heal all manner of illnesses. The pentacle should be used when there is a threat of death to preserve life.

3) The third pentacle is used to incite wrath and discord, among others. It is powered with the knowledge and strength to encourage those who hide behind the veil of religion to hurt you and show you their true colors. It defends the operator with magical and physical forces to subjugate the evil and dark spirits that threaten to attack.

4) The fourth pentacle gives the operator great virtue and vindication in battle. It releases a force that can be used to demolish any adversary and subdue the demonic forces that are sent to destroy us.

5) The fifth pentacle has the power to literally "take the breath" away from your adversaries. Evil is terrorized by the sight of this pentacle and will retreat, defeated by its power.

6) The sixth pentacle is the ultimate shield against evil. It has such a strong defensive quality that it can fend off any magical or psychic invasion. Call upon this pentacle when all other resources have been exhausted.

7) The seventh pentacle has the power to bring the most powerful forces of nature down upon your enemy's heads. Smote them with rain, hail, and flaming fires from the heat of the sun or the strength of the wind until they lie broken and defeated by nature.

The **Jupiter Pentacles** have seven different designs that are associated with them:

1) The first pentacle attracts wealth and success to businesses. Parasiel, the lord of treasures, is featured on the pentacle and governs the power of wealth and glory.

2) The second pentacle brings the bearer success and wealth accompanied by peace of mind. It is used by people who are uncomfortable with sudden wealth or success, and it can help bring a sense of acceptance and wellbeing. It creates a stillness within that promotes the feeling of entitlement to your success.

3) The third pentacle helps the user protect their home and keep it free from evil and dark spirits. The pentacle also has the power to send blessings of light to people who are far away.

4) The fourth pentacle encourages wealth and riches to be attracted to the bearer. The bearer can expect much wealth and success to manifest along with the power to maintain their levels of prosperity.

5) The fifth pentacle encourages the user to connect with the Universe and become the recipient of visions. It gives you the power to align your views with those residing in different realms and combine the knowledge you receive.

6) The sixth pentacle should be used by people who feel vulnerable and at risk from dark forces. It gives them the power to recharge and use the elements of nature to protect themselves.

7) The seventh pentacle dispels the causes of poverty and deprivation. It drives away the spirits that guard fortunes and makes them discoverable by mortals. It has the power to raise people from the mire and make them into successful functioning members of society. Invoking this pentacle will help those who have lost a job or found themselves impoverished.

The Saturn Pentacles have seven different designs associated with them:

1) The first pentacle is of great value for striking terror into the hearts of spirits. Use this to protect yourself and send malignant beings scurrying away.

2) The second pentacle will make your enemies shameful and strip them of their pride.

3) The third pentacle speaks directly to the essence of Saturn and should be invoked at night or maximum power. Use it to connect to Saturn's energy to rid yourself of disappointment and despair.

4) The fourth pentacle governs the power of destruction and chaos. It serves to connect you to spirits who have news and information that will aid your magical works.

5) The fifth pentacle removes the spirits that guard treasures. These can be physical or spiritual treasures depending on your needs. Invoke them and gain access to what you need.

6) The sixth pentacle is a powerful tool to pronounce the name of whomever you wish to be possessed by demons. The spirits have the power to render them possessed by demons, so they pose no threat to you or your family.

7) The seventh pentacle has the power to invoke earthquakes and make the world tremble with force.

These pentacles or seals can be invoked by using Psalms from the Bible, but some people prefer to use more modern methods to activate their pentacles with text from a variety of different beliefs. The key thing to remember is that you are the person in charge, and you decide what works for you.

The History of the Solomonic Texts

The books date back to the 14th or 15th century and are purportedly written by King Solomon, also called Jedidiah, a fabulously wealthy and wise king whose deeds were recorded in the Old Testament. Several versions of Solomon's teachings appeared in the same era when Renaissance magick was becoming more prominent.

King Solomon is one of 48 Hebrew prophets, but history has elevated him to the Major Prophet of God, who was the keeper of the greatest knowledge regarding the supernatural world and the entities that dwell there. He was given this knowledge by an angel sent by God, who was considered the Most High representative. King Solomon was the first mortal ordained by God to share his divine wisdom of the esoteric and ethereal energies and how to identify the cosmic forms of existence.

The Keys of Solomon is a comprehensive guide to the magical connections between the planets, the almighty God, and the energies that bind us all. We have only touched briefly on the contents to study how the pentacles can form part of our protection, but the Keys of Solomon contain so much information that it takes years of study to understand them. They are the font of spiritual knowledge and help us understand how light overpowers darkness just as wisdom reigns supreme.

Activating Your Pentacle

There are some things to consider when you are preparing your pentacle for use. In the past, the seals were made from metal specific to the planetary association it came from. However, we may now be more flexible with the materials we use. Modern witches use the relevant colors, days, and times to prepare their pentacles but use other materials to produce the pentacle. A printed image of the pentacle isn't as traditional, but it is easier to produce and more practical. Nobody expects you to use the traditional metals as they can be hard to get hold of, especially mercury, as it is poisonous.

Knowing the appropriate days and colors will help you prepare for the consecration of your chosen pentacle.

Moon is associated with Monday, Silver, and Silver

Mercury is associated with Wednesday, Mixed colors, and Mercury

Venus is associated with Friday, Green, and Copper

Sun id associated with Sunday, Yellow and Gold

Mars is associated with Tuesday, Red, and Iron

Jupiter is associated with Thursday, Blue, and Tin

Saturn is associated with Saturday, Black, and Lead

The Consecration Ritual

Prepare by taking a shower or a ritual bath. The petitioner will be better received by the gods when they are clean both physically and spiritually. Make yourself presentable to the deities, and they will look favorably on you.

Petition the Gods

Take a piece of paper and draw two circles with a marker pen corresponding to your chosen planetary pentacle—for instance, black ink for Saturn and red ink for Mars. Call upon the god that represents your intent. Some people use the gods of Egypt, Greece, or Hebrew origin, while some prefer the more contemporary gods. Research your choices for better results.

Gods who punish evil can include Ganesha, Hanuman, Murugan, and Shiva

Gods who will give mercy can include Anubis, Dagda, Govinda, and Vishnu

Gods who bestow blessings can include Sunna, Osiris, Krishna, and Eros

Place the image of your chosen pentacle(s) in the double circle.

Face East and purify your pentacles and seal with the smoke of an incense stick. Myrrh, Frankincense, cedarwood, or rosemary work well.

Read your favorite psalms or prayers as you cleanse the pentacles. Choose readings that correspond to your intent and desires.

Compose an Oration Spell

There is fixed text in chapter eight of the Key of Solomon, but it is quite rigid and based on Biblical figures, including Moses and Abraham. This is fine if you are a Christian, but the pentacles work for all religions and beliefs. Your oration can include your beliefs, your gods, and your inner strength.

Once you have finished the oration, hold the pentacle in your left hand and recite a psalm or your own prayer to activate the seal ready for use.

The pentacles can be recharged on the days representing them and should be anointed and blessed at least once a week.

Create Your Own Grimoire

We have already discussed how important it is to keep a journal of your magical practices because you need to know how you are progressing. The Wiccan concept of the traditional grimoire is often known as a Book of Shadows, but the principles are the same. You can incorporate your journal into a modern grimoire, or you can keep it separate; the choice is yours.

Every magician is different, and your grimoire will reflect that. The following are some examples of what you could include:

- Phases of the moon and how they affect your spells
- Cleansing spells
- Incantations and their power
- Herbs and how to use them
- Crystals and their power
- Attraction spells
- How to use tarot cards in magick
- How to invoke elementals
- Potions for love, wealth, and banishing
- Laws of your tradition
- Gods and Goddesses
- How to prepare magick tools
- The dedication used by your coven
- The Wheel of the Year and what it means to the spells you cast
- Sacred texts and alphabets

The list is endless, and you can make your book as diverse as you like. Use illustrations and text to make it a personal journal of your magick. Use a three-ring binder so you can create sections and move your information around to different sections. Magick is like any other form of learning - it is fluid and needs to grow. Your grimoire should be filled with your experiences and information so you can turn to it whenever you need help and inspiration.

The grimoire should grow in size as you grow in experience and confidence. Consider it a diary with a reference section that helps you every single day. Your grimoire should be kept in a safe place where other people can't access it or see its contents.

Chapter 9: Angelic Protection

Angels and Archangels have been guiding and protecting humans since the beginning of time. Most are depicted as ethereal beings dressed in white robes with impressive wings. These images may have originated from the Greek deities like Nike and Eros, but almost every culture in the world has some form of angelic being whose job is to convey messages between the Divine and the physical realm.

Primitive societies often depicted animal-like beings that hover between the two realms. Indigenous cultures often believed that spirits of animals and humans became blessed messengers and guardian spirits. They built totem poles and other symbolic images to celebrate their association with these angelic beings.

The Ancient world preferred their messengers to take a god-like form and were charged with specific tasks and areas of expertise. Although some were depicted with wings, they were not angels per se, more like gods who carried messages.

Eastern Religions

Hinduism and Buddhism had spiritual facilitators known as Devas, who inhabited the higher plane but could interact with mortals. They were more likely to ride enchanted chariots or horses rather than flying as they didn't have wings like most angelic beings. Buddhists believe that communing with the Deva is only achievable by those who are fully spiritually awakened.

The Tennin were sylph-like creatures in Japan and China, clad in brightly colored kimonos with feather decorations. They exist in tales where they visit Earth, fall in love with a human, marry them, and then return to their own reality after their identity is uncovered. Shintoists believe in the Kami, or spirits associated with natural phenomena such as rivers and canyons.

Christianity

The representation of angels as we know them with human personalities and powers to help us live a better life originated in Christianity. Religious art from mosaics found in catacombs forms some of the first images of winged beings alongside birds communicating with God. Baroque ceiling art further embellished the image with distinct facial features and well-sculpted bodies.

Between the late 1550s and the 1700s, angels became popular subjects for the European artists of the age. The art was inseparably linked with the Catholic Church who used the artists' work to promote the opulence and wealth of the organization. The subject matter often included the Virgin Mary, Saints, and stories from the Bible, so the inclusion of angels was a natural progression.

Summoning Angels and Archangels

When you need help from above, sometimes a simple prayer that comes from the heart is enough. They are always listening and will come to your aid whenever you need them. But what if you need specific help and are seeking a more intense connection? If you want to enhance your life by involving the heavenly host, then you have to ask! You can wait for them to turn up of their own volition but speeding up the process will help you feel empowered and in control. The different angels and archangels all have specific powers, so you can target the ones you feel will be most helpful.

Angelic beings are benevolent and eager to help humans. We base our knowledge on Christian theology, but it is also backed up by more arcane teachings such as the Kabbalah, where angels are part of the Tree of Life and demons reside in the Tree of Knowledge. Both kinds of spirits have attributes that can enhance our lives and help us to improve.

Understanding the Difference between an Angel and a Guardian Angel

Guardian angels are the highest benevolent entity apart from God himself. Invoking them is a long and difficult process and should only be undertaken by expert magicians. There are rituals available for summoning them, but they are dangerous and take years to complete. Although angels and archangels sound like elevated beings, and they are, they are much more accessible to mere humans. Guardian angels should not be confused with guardian spirits, who are much more accessible.

What Do the Archangels Do?

There are 17 Archangels in most teachings, but some religions think there are more than this. Although the Bible only refers to Archangels twice in the scriptures, they have unimaginable powers that can help humankind fight evil and demons.

Archangels were created to oversee the heavenly host and guide them in their constant fight with spiritual warfare. Archangels are everywhere, and once you accept their presence, you can begin to reap the rewards of their bounties.

Who Are the Archangels?

Archangel Michael

The principle of light - most people believe he is God's right-hand man and his chief protector. Michael is a dragon slayer and the champion of the skies, protecting you from psychic attacks and astral debris. When the Day of Judgement arrives, he is in charge of weighing human souls to determine if they will pass into eternity.

Archangel Gabriel

Best known for his role in conveying God's message to Mary, Gabriel is the chief communications officer who can help you receive and understand messages from the Divine. Call on him when you need to see things clearly and commune with higher beings.

Archangel Metatron

The angel of life. He will help you raise your vibrations and make important decisions. He is the angel that records heavenly happenings and is incredibly organized and calm. He helps children make that troubled transition from childhood to adulthood.

Archangel Raphael

The healing angel. He is the patron of the sick and works closely with people involved in the medical industry. His compassion and caring side mean he can help with all kinds of trauma - physical, emotional, and spiritual. Raphael deals with kids who are ill and helps them find relief. If you are dealing with any kind of illness or need guidance, call upon him for help.

Archangel Ariel

The Lioness of God. She is the guardian of injured animals and will heal them and protect them from further harm. She oversees the natural world and will help you overcome any trauma associated with natural disasters. If you feel an affinity with nature and are passionate about environmental issues, call on Ariel for her patronage.

Archangel Haniel

She is the protector of souls and will help you improve your spiritual communication skills. Haniel is especially in tune with female energies and can help females find relief when they are experiencing their monthly cycles. Haniel can help you achieve clairvoyance powers and fulfill your higher purpose. Don't hesitate to call her; she loves to help.

Archangel Jophiel

The Beauty of God. Jophiel is the angel of beauty and wisdom. She is blessed with high vibrational energy and works with creative souls to find their muse and creative inspirations. If you are experiencing chaotic thoughts or negative emotions, Jophiel can bring calm and tranquility to your life. If you feel lost, call on Jophiel to guide you safely home.

Archangel Muriel

The Perfume of God. Muriel is a supportive entity who is attuned to emotions and intuitively knows when people need compassion. She is blessed with emotional strength and can be called upon to help when you doubt yourself and need guidance. She is a compassionate soul who will listen to you and give you the help you need.

Archangel Uriel

The fire of God. Uriel is the illuminated seraphim who stands by God's side and lights the path to spiritual insight. He is considered one of the wisest archangels and has the ear of the Creator himself. If you seek to raise your personal vibrations or become more attuned to the spirit realm, reach out to Uriel for his help and guidance. He will help you when you find yourself lost and confused because he is the light that penetrates even the darkest place.

Archangel Azrael

The angel of death. While his association with death may seem sinister, remember that spiritually death represents rebirth as well as mortal endings. Azrael will help you if you have experienced grief or if you are preparing to lose someone. He will get you through difficult times and give you the support to emerge, reborn following your grief and sorrow. Call upon him to strengthen your prayers or meditations.

Archangel Zadkiel

The angel of forgiveness and mercy, Zadkiel, has the power to help you move on from difficult periods of your life. He teaches you how to purge negativity from your spirit so you can move on without being held back by ties from the past. If you have trouble forgiving people who have wronged you, Zadkiel will help you resolve your emotions.

Archangel Chamuel

The angel of peaceful relationships. If you struggle to find your place in the world, call on Chamuel to inspire you to make solid connections and ties. Chamuel is the expert on inner peace and knows how to connect you to the Divine beings so you can grow and become spiritually strong. You will know when he has heard your call for help as you will feel a butterfly sensation in your gut.

Archangel Jeremiel

The angel of presence. Jeremiel was one of the seven original archangels chosen by God to serve humanity, so he has an innate sense of how humanity works. Unlike his other archangel counterparts, he doesn't communicate directly with humans. Instead, he uses symbols, mental images, visions, and dreams. He is the merciful face of the Divine beings and will work tirelessly to help you become aware of the power of your emotions and thoughts. He translates the messages from the ether into relatable images and dreams so you can understand even the most complex instructions.

Archangel Raziel

The angel of secrets. Raziel understands that mortals need to communicate with God, and he agrees that the other angels should work to make that happen. He also understands that if God is too accessible, he loses some of his power. Raziel is the keeper of the enigma when it comes to God, and he guards his place with honor. That doesn't mean he won't work with us; he just does it silently and stays undercover. Ask Raziel for help, and he will assist you even though you may not be aware of his presence. He will make you do the work and learn from your mistakes, but he will always ensure every effort is repaid with psychic power.

Archangel Sandalphon

The guardian of nature. When it comes to mankind, Sandalphon, one of the most easygoing archangels, is gentle and patient. He's used to interacting with animals and nature, so he understands why some people feel apprehensive. His down-to-earth attitude makes him more approachable, and he is usually the first archangel people invoke.

Archangel Sachiel

The angel of success. Sachiel is a mysterious angel and has kept his light hidden for generations but is now more connected to Earth and humans. He helps people achieve success, which can lead to material gain and wealth. You may think this is a strange path for angelic beings, but the angels know that being rewarded for effort isn't a sin. Sachiel is associated with the planet Jupiter that represents growth, evolution, and risks. All these elements are needed if success and expansion are to follow.

Archangel Orion

The angel of manifestation. Named after Orion, one of the brightest stars in the universe, you may think this archangel is ostentatious and shines bright in the firmament. Quite the contrary. When Orion is close, he emits a low-level vibration, yet he will encourage you to settle your inner conflicts and accomplish your dreams.

Who Can Benefit from Archangels?

Archangels are unconcerned with their religious affiliations. They are dedicated to helping all persons, not just Christians. Since the beginning of time, their power has existed, and celestial visits come to those who need them. They will never harm you because their force is infused with divine love and healing. Even though they are in the skies, we are always connected to them because their love binds us all.

They care about your positivity, spiritual well-being, and inner peace, and all you have to do to benefit from their presence is be open to the concept that Archangels can and will assist you. Of course, you can speed the process up or make it more powerful by invoking the archangel(s) of your choice to help you with specific needs.

How to Invoke Archangels

Angelic Sign Ritual

Each archangel has a sign or symbol associated with it. Michael is associated with the star sapphire or the scales of justice. Gabriel is associated with white lilies or the moon, while Uriel is associated with horns of plenty.

Choose the archangel you want to work with and choose a sign with which they are associated. Draw it on a piece of paper and surround the picture with three white candles. Make the rest of the room dark, so only the candlelight shines.

Gaze at the image until it becomes three-dimensional. Feel the energy shift as you become aware of the change you feel in your breathing. The figure may even begin to float above the paper as the energy levels change and become charged.

Commit the image to memory and store it away for the next time you need it. As you develop your practice, it will become easier to conjure your archangel without the aid of candles and paper. You will have formed a bond that will stay with you forever.

Angelic Mantra

The archangels understand the significance of their given names. God has given them a name, which is the highest honor conferred upon any spiritual being. Repeating their name is a simple way to summon them. Find a good environment where you won't disturb or be disturbed by others.

First, repeat their name silently for ten minutes to form a bond. Now, begin to chant. Feel the power of their name as you chant it, and increase the volume as your connection forms and strengthens. You will know when it's time to stop because you will feel their presence with you.

Angelic Prayer

Prayer is one of the most powerful tools you have. Even if you aren't religious, your prayer is a statement that comes from the heart, and that is what the angels are seeking. Heartfelt emotions and deep sincerity are like bright lights and will attract them to your side.

Prayers are important because they don't just appeal to the archangels; they can also tell them what you seek from them.

For instance, if you seek help from Raphael for healing matters, try composing something like this:

Oh, mighty Raphael, the healer of the skies, I ask for your guidance

Help me find strength and fortitude to deal with my physical ailments

Bring spiritual strength to my side so I can emerge from illness as a healthy spirit

Bestow on me the power of fire to increase my energy and make any journey less tiring

I want to feel the power of the Divine and find comfort in it.

Great Raphael, I devote myself to your power and wisdom

Repeat his name as a mantra until you feel comfortable you have been heard.

Your prayer could be completely different and use more direct language. It doesn't matter to the archangels as they recognize when someone is sincere and needs their help. Sincerity matters more than any fancy words or prayers.

Summoning an angel can be a different matter. Archangels are charged with keeping us safe and spiritually healthy, but what if you need help with minor issues. Some spells summon angels to help you do more mundane tasks and solve everyday issues.

Angel spells help you with whatever you need. Weight loss, growing your hair, finding a new job, getting your partner to listen to you, the list is endless, and nothing is too trivial to invoke angels to help you.

Simple Angel Invocation

Stand at your altar or any other special and private place. Place a bell on your face and turn to the skies. Ask the angels for help, for instance, "I love my life, but I wish to make it better, help me see clearer ways to eat healthily and exercise more." Now, ring your bell once. Turn to the East and repeat the chant with another ring of the bell. Complete the four points of the compass before returning to your original position. Repeat the phrase once more and ring your bell nine times.

Performing your invocation under the light of the full moon will make it more powerful.

The simple thing to take away from this chapter is that the angels and Archangels are powerful beings who are there for us. Imagine a host of heavenly beings working on your behalf - doesn't that make you feel powerful and capable of everything? Go ahead and begin your angel quest. You are worth it!

Chapter 10: Planetary Magick for Protection

Planetary magick has its roots in Hermeticism, which teaches us that we exist in the center of a planetary paradigm that affects how we exist on Earth. The structure of the paradigm resembles an onion and can be viewed in two different ways. As humans, you can begin to contemplate the layers of consciousness from the center or the outside in from the Divine perspective.

The spheres' connection to the human consciousness forms the perspective that governs the Kabbalah Tree of Life, which is important for understanding the evolution of consciousness and how the Sephiroth is central to our being. For magical purposes, a more balanced view of the planets is needed. This helps us choose what planets will influence our works and make them successful.

Every witch or magical practitioner is different. Your birthday, the time you were born, and the zodiac sign that governs you are all important. Your character is a major factor in how you practice magick and what elements and planets influence you. Nobody can tell you what path to take when it comes to magick, so the more knowledge you have, the more informed decisions you can make.

Planetary Magick

Working with the main planets in the solar system will give you the chance to work with powerful forces and tap into the elemental energies they contain. For decades, witches have been associated with the moon, and it is well known that magick works best when conducted within the appropriate lunar cycle. Common logic says that the other solar bodies in our cosmos are equally powerful and should be used to enhance spells and magical activities.

Magick should be fluid and ready to embrace energy and power from all sources, so combining complementary elements and the power of the individual solar sources can only heighten the power of our magick. Connect and interact with the planets by integrating your spell work with the elements that relate to them daily. Write down your works and how successful they are in your journal to form an overview of what works for you and what doesn't.

Each of the planets is represented by a glyph, an esoteric symbol that originates from the term "to carve," and there are many representations of these online. Research them and choose what symbol and glyph appeal to you for each of your planets. Print them or draw them onto a chart to begin your connection with the planets and their magical properties.

Celestial deities govern the planetary intelligence of each sphere, so remember that you are connecting with a higher being, and you need to win their favors. Offerings and meditation will show your intention to establish a connection, so choose them carefully. Get to know the deities that are associated with each celestial body and address them directly.

The Moon

Let's begin with the most familiar planet we are used to working with. The Moon is the planet of family and familial ties. Casting spells as it waxes will increase your influence over family matters and bring you all together. The waning moon is the perfect time to cast banishment spells to stop disagreements and conflict. Lunar energy can be used to promote clairvoyance and perception while increasing self-development and spiritual growth. The Moon has a feminine quality and will bring power to fertility spells.

Moon Correspondences

- Magick number - 9
- Zodiac sign - Cancer
- Element - Water
- Colors - White and Silver
- Metal - Silver
- Preferred Day - Monday
- Stones and crystals - Smoky quartz, black obsidian, selenite, Labradorian
- Plants and herbs - Lemon balm rose, wild oats, laurel lavender
- Incense - Lavender, jasmine, violet, lotus
- Animals - Wolf, Bat, Moth, Owls, Rats
- Gods - Lasya, Luna, Selene, Diana, Hathor
- Archangel - Gabriel

Mars

Sexuality, self-worth, and charisma are all represented by this planet. If you wish to boost your energy and take more risks, work with Mars. It will instill courage, confidence, and a greater sense of competition in you, allowing you to succeed in your career. Warriors often invoked Mars to give them strength in battle, so tap into your inner warrior and call on Mars to assist you in your struggles. Mars can help you with potency and passion spells if your relationship is in crisis.

Mars Correspondences

- Magick number - 5
- Zodiac sign - Aries
- Element - Fire
- Colors - Red
- Metal - Iron
- Preferred day - Tuesday

- Stones and crystals - Ruby, garnet, bloodstone, jasper, amethyst
- Plants and herbs - Peppers, capers, nettles, ginseng, cayenne, grape root
- Incense - Tobacco, basil, pepper
- Animals - Horse, woodpecker, lions, bears, tigers
- Gods - Mars, Minerva, Flora, Ares, Juno
- Archangel - Michael

Mercury

In astral magick, Mercury is the planet of success. It will help you achieve your wildest dreams and overcome obstacles. Use it to influence spells before job interviews or court appearances. It has the energy needed to be successful in business and commerce while strengthening your language skills and the ability to communicate successfully. It has heightened qualities for the acquisition of knowledge and mental expansion.

Mercury Correspondences

- Magical number - 8
- Zodiac sign - Gemini and Virgo
- Element - Air and water
- Colors - Orange Indigo, violet, yellow, purple
- Metal - Quicksilver
- Preferred day - Wednesday
- Stones and crystals - Black tourmaline, blue kyanite, rainbow fluorite, agate, aventurine
- Plants and herbs - Ash, celery, chickweed, dill, fennel, garlic mustard, hazel
- Incense - Storax, clary, sage, moss
- Animals - Dogs, monkeys, apes, eagles
- Gods - Ganesha, Hermes, Buddha, Loki, Thoth, Glooskap
- Archangel - Raphael

Jupiter

Jupiter is the king of the gods in planetary magick, and he may bestow incredibly good fortune and luck on your efforts. It is the ultimate protector, bestowing prosperity, wealth, and abundance upon those who invoke its powers. Use the energy to become grounded and stable when you are feeling adrift and need self-development.

Jupiter Correspondences

- Magical number - 4
- Zodiac signs - Sagittarius and Pisces
- Elements - Air and fire
- Colors - Blue, violet, yellow, indigo, green
- Metal - Tin
- Stones and crystals - Sapphire, amethyst, emerald, marble, topaz
- Plants and herbs - Figs, hyssop, sage, magnolia, cinquefoil, oak
- Incense Cedar - sage magnolia, saffron
- Animals - Eagles, Giraffes, horses, jackals, cats
- Gods - Thor, Jove, Zeus, Abundantia
- Archangel - Uriel

Venus

Associated with love and beauty, you could be fooled into thinking this planet's energies are concerned with frivolous matters. While Venus is connected with love, lust, and passion spells, it is also the planet associated with legal matters. Venus's energy will make you more resolute and discerning with your decisions when you sign legal documents or form contracts.

A combination of energies from this planet will promote your creativity, your artistic inclinations, and your joy of life. Use it in spells for fertility and growth.

Venus Correspondences

- Magical number - 7
- Element - Air
- Colors - Green, red, gold
- Metal - Copper
- Preferred day - Friday
- Stones and crystals - Emerald, diamonds, quartz, topaz
- Plants and herbs - Rose, thyme, myrtle, bergamot
- Incense - Rose, Ylang, sandalwood, bergamot
- Animals - Dove, cheetah, goose, hyena
- Gods - Venus, Kamadeva, Himeros, Eros, Anteros
- Archangel - Haniel

Sun

Call on the Sun's energy when you are casting spells for harmony and peace. When you want to make new starts and friendships, her warmth and light will show you the way to go. The energies that come from the Sun are vital, regenerative, stable yet volatile.

Sun Correspondences

- Magical number - 6
- Zodiac sign - Leo
- Element - Fire
- Colors - Gold, yellow, orange, red
- Metal - Gold
- Preferred day - Sunday
- Stones and crystals - Tiger eye, Citrine, Ametrine, Sunstone, quartz
- Plants and herbs - Sunflowers, St. John's Wort, basil, anise, daisy, clover
- Incense - Frankincense, sage, cinnamon, rose
- Animals - Lion, eagle, griffin, dove, pig, tortoise

- Gods - Ra, Tonatiuh, Surya, Apollo, Shamash
- Archangel - Michael

Pluto

Pluto has hidden depths that can assist you in uncovering some of the secrets and knowledge you seek. Invoke Pluto to boost the potency of your rebirth, transformation, and relationship-improvement spells. Pluto is the planet of karma and justice, and its magical energies will help you.

Pluto Correspondences

- Magical number - 0
- Zodiac signs - Cancer and Scorpio
- Element - Water
- Colors - Brown, black, grey, umber
- Preferred day - Tuesday
- Stones and crystals - Black opal, black tourmaline, jet, garnet, hematite, citrine, moldavite
- Plants and herbs - Nettle, oak, truffles, cypress
- Gods - Kalfu, Terminus, Zigu, Pluto, Osiris
- Archangel – Gabriel

Uranus

Madness, insanity, and genius are all associated with Uranus. Uranus is the ruling planet of innovators. People who are willing to push boundaries and venture beyond their comfort zones. If you believe your work has gotten too conventional, ask Uranus to broaden your horizons. It has the power to make you feel more cheerful, less uptight, and inspired to be more creative. Change the way you think about creation and art by using its associations.

Uranus Correspondences

- Magical number - 4
- Zodiac signs - Aquarius and Gemini
- Element - Air

- Colors - White, green, purple, indigo, yellow
- Metal - White gold, platinum,
- Preferred day - Wednesday
- Chakras - Crown throat
- Stones and crystals - Quartz, Citrine, hematite, sunstone
- Plants and herbs - Dill, rowan, ash, rosemary
- Gods - Isis, Ganesh, Thor, Odin, Cupid, Anat

Neptune

Neptune is often regarded as the planet most suited for the occultist. Its energy encourages the user to become more skilled in dream works, psychic communication, and visions. It works well with Uranus to form a deeper connection to the spirit world. Use it to dissolve boundaries and travel freely on all planes of existence.

Neptune Correspondences

- Magical number - 6
- Zodiac signs – Pisces, Aquarius
- Element - Water
- Colors - Indigo, pink, coral, purple, aquamarine
- Metal - Platinum
- Preferred day - Friday
- Stones and crystals - Jade, emerald, tourmaline, opal, coral, mother of pearl
- Plants and herbs - Wild Sea fennel, samphire, celery, rosemary, and sea moss
- Gods - Neptune, Poseidon, Long Wang, Demeter
- Magical association - Mermaids, Sylphs

Saturn

There is one planet that isn't listed above, and that is Saturn. The last of the ancient planets was the farthest point that ancient astrologers could see. They classed it as the Greater Malefic because it had associations with death and darkness. They believed that nothing existed beyond Saturn and the planet was the harbinger of death. At the time, the average age span of humans was around thirty years which was also the life span of Saturn.

The thirty-year cycle that Saturn undergoes does have relevance today, but it is much more positive. Today, we recognize that our life can be defined by thirty-year cycles as we enter new phases of maturity. Have you ever noticed how crazy people get about turning thirty? It is a birthday that seems to make us confront our past and what lessons we have learned before going forward into the new cycle. In astrological terms, you aren't deemed to be a fully formed adult until you have lived as long as a cycle of the planet Saturn.

As the last of the inner planets, Saturn is the limit of the known realm, and all the planets that lie beyond it have relevantly modern history. Magick can be defined in much the same way - some people prefer the older, more traditional methods while others revel in the new methods available. The rings of Saturn are a perfect representation of how chaos can be governed by gravity to form disciplined and well-ordered rings of great beauty and strength. The ice and rocks that form the rings of Saturn were original without order until the formation of the solar system, which resulted in their formation. Saturn is the power and functionality that represents structure and order.

Saturn, like Jupiter, has an impressive Moon system. The largest of the ten moons is the size of Mercury, giving it significant spiritual weight. Saturn's gravitational pull allows it to contract and places it in the solar system's upper octave. A cross on top of a crescent moon symbolizes it, and it is thought to be the planet most related to karma.

Saturn has connections with the crown and root chakra, which gives it opposing powers relating to earthly challenges and in the realm of higher consciousness. Saturn acts as a teacher, but it takes a hands-on approach to the lessons it teaches. Rather than instruct people how to face challenges and obstacles they face in their earthly existence, it manifests them and forces them to face their fears. Saturn's instructions start as a faint inner voice, but you will bear the consequences if you disregard them. The metal counterpart of Saturn is lead, which represents the weight of responsibility that humans bear during their lifetime on Earth.

In Kabbalah, Saturn is linked to feminine energy, which gives it the power to be the ultimate cosmic goddess, while its links with the Greek gods mean it is seen as the epitome of Fatherhood. Combining this primal power with the ancient beliefs means Saturn is the Ancient Father and Mother to us all. Saturn has many divine faces, and during the winter solstice, it has powers of rebirth that are intrinsically linked with the divine child. Saturn is the embodiment of family and the ties that bind them and keep them safe.

When you call on Saturn, you are invoking a unique form of protection. When Mars is invoked, you benefit from the power of the warrior and arm yourself for a fight. When Saturn becomes involved, you are neutralizing a situation and protecting yourself with the power to banish and inhibit your enemies rather than destroy them. Put simply, if a bullet were heading your way, the power of Saturn would slow it before bringing it to the ground.

When used in ritual magick, the power of Saturn is a balanced and organized force. It will help you be more disciplined when you need to complete a task or stay on a certain path. It will also assist you in understanding why certain actions are required and the benefits you might expect.

The power of Saturn can be used in any spell or ritual that requires a manifestation on the physical plane. It is especially powerful for success and prosperity through your career, helping you use your magick to understand how to manipulate authority and corporate structures to climb the career ladder. Remember that Saturn is the planet of karma and will not allow you to use its power to cause harm to others. It will teach you how to become successful without treading on others.

Saturn Correspondences

- Magical number - 7
- Element - Earth

- Preferred day - Saturday
- Colors - Black, navy blue, dark brown, amber
- Stones and crystals - Onyx, black tourmaline, obsidian, jet
- Incense - Binak oil, cypress, spruce, thyme, sulfur
- Plants and herbs - Ash, belladonna, comfrey, daffodil, elm, hemlock, Lenten rose, pansy, rowan, tobacco, willow
- Gods - Erebos, Set, Hodr, Ahriman, Ah Puch

The rituals and magick are associated with career, self-control, endurance, longevity, property matters, and land management.

Propitiation Ritual of Saturn

The power of Saturn can be summoned by using this ritual to gain the goodwill of this powerful force. Timing is essential, but the cycle of Saturn can be lengthy, and the ideal day may be years away. If you use your birthday as a guide, it is easier to define a more accessible day of Saturn. Choose a Saturday within 52 days of your birthday to mark the completion of your one-year cycle, with each day representing one week. Reflect on how you have felt spiritually in the last year and what you hope to achieve in the next.

Arrange your altar with a hexagram that has the glyph of Saturn at its center. Decorate the altar with any lead talismans you have or the names of your favorite deities. Use a modern script or Hebrew text to state your intentions.

What you will need:

- Six white tea lights
- A larger black candle or an oil lamp with a new wick
- Sesame oil mixed with 3 drops of myrrh
- A jar of naturally sourced water from a stream, river, or well
- Myrrh resin
- A mixture of sea salt, black rice, and sesame seeds
- Prayer beads for chanting (optional)
- Crystal glasses, fireproof bowl, charcoal

The hour of Saturn should be calculated by consulting charts available online before the ritual takes place. Before the planetary hour, the candles should be arranged to represent the six other planets with the larger candle or oil lamp in the center. These candles should be in the center of your altar with their individual glyphs identifying them, although this is optional as the focus of your ritual is Saturn. Fill your glasses separately with the water and the dry mixture and place them at the side of the candle/lamp.

At the start of the planetary hour, light each of the tea lights with an invocation to the separate planets they represent.

> 1) I light this candle to the Moon, and I recognize the need to hear her sweet, pure voice in my magick.
>
> 2) I light this candle for Mercury and ask that he communicates with me clearly and sharply.
>
> 3) I light this candle to Venus, a pure and resonating force.
>
> 4) I light this candle to the Sun; I welcome her warm and holy voice in my life.
>
> 5) I light this candle to Mars; I ask that he communicates with me in strength and honor.
>
> 6) I light this candle to Jupiter, whose royal voice shall speak to me and fill me with joy.

Use a wand or your finger to link the energies of the six planets to your central source before lighting the myrrh incense and the lamp of Saturn. Dedicate the light to Saturn.

I light this lamp and dedicate it to the Lord Saturn, who shines his celestial being into our lives to guide and enlighten us. He illuminates our paths and gives us the strength to follow them. Continue to keep us safe and protect us from harm.

Dedicate the Incense to Saturn

I burn this myrrh to create a spiritual smoke that will rise and fill this place in the glory of Saturn. Bestow upon us your sweet heavenly smoke and fill our voids, spirits, and souls with your heavenly blessings.

Dedicate the Water to Saturn

I present this natural liquid to Lord Saturn as a symbol of my connection to the earth and the purity of my intentions. We ask that you bless us with your cleansing spirit and wash away all evil and pollution from our lives. Remove our obstacles and clear the path for success.

Dedicate the Dry Mix to Saturn

I offer this salt mix to Saturn to represent the strength he holds over our hearts and minds. Strengthen us with your nourishment and knowledge, so we can face the world enlightened and with the power to grow.

Now, you can make the ritual as personal as you like. Choose a mantra, prayer, or incantation to repeat as you use your set of prayer beads, or you can simply end the ritual and extinguish the lamp of Saturn. Let the other candles burn out safely on their own and thank the Lord Saturn for his time and attention. Now, clean yourself physically and spiritually to make sure your ritual has a balanced outcome. Saturn's energy can be intense, so it's important to maintain a feeling of control.

Planetary magick is a powerful part of your spiritual journey. Use this knowledge to guide you through the solar system and the energies you will find there.

Conclusion

Everyone is aware of the dangers we encounter daily. We'll never be completely safe, but we may be properly protected and vigilant anyway. Use what you've learned in this book. You'll have a high level of protection when you enter the spiritual realms, perform sacred rituals, and cast spells while being protected by a variety of energies. They will keep you safe in your work if you use them with respect.

Part 2: Enochian Magic

Unlock the Secrets of the Book of Enoch, Ceremonial Magick, Nephilim, Fallen Angels, Archangels, Angelic Sigils, Kabbalah, and Invocation

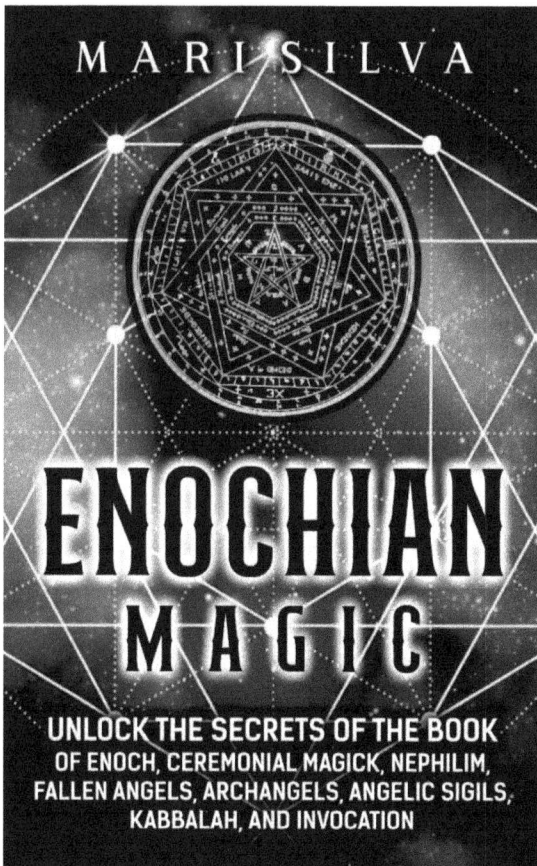

Introduction

Magic is a wonderful thing. You can invoke the essence of the Divine Creator or connect with angels. You can command angels, demons, and every other spirit in between. With Enochian magic, you will be able to express yourself spiritually and feed the part of you that many other people often ignore. You can use magic to make your life more magical. If you know this already, then here's something else: there's no better way to practice than Enochian magic.

Ceremonial magic is a good way to realize the truth about who you really are and why you're here. Discovering your purpose will help you feel more fulfilled and make your life that much more awesome. Aleister Crowley, the great magician who lived from 1875 to 1947, once said that magic is about causing changes in your life that conform with your will, and he was completely correct. The only way to get the changes you desire is through magic and your will. It's a personal process, where you seek not to change the world around you but instead, yourself. As you change, the world around you is forced to follow suit.

Enochian magic was named after the Biblical Enoch, a prophet who walked closely with God, so much so it's said he knew the deepest secrets and mysteries that even in this day and age we seek. This is a wonderful and the most powerful magic system yet, based on the many years of work put in by John Dee and Edward Kelley. The magic they brought us is the foundation of many other forms of magic that you may be more familiar with. So, if you choose to work with Enochian magic, you will be drinking straight from the source. This book will give you the truth, straight up, so you too can follow this path.

In this book, you're going to discover the world of Enochian magic. You will learn the curious tale of how a man who once sought the divine secret of the universe, just like you are doing now, found himself communicating with the very beings who were here before here was a place and before time ever existed. You'll learn the significance of the magical tools, the rites that make up Enochian magic and develop a healthy respect for how it's come to be what it is today.

You're about to read the very secrets of the universe, which you can use to hack your reality and make it what you know it should be. However, it's one thing to read about Enochian magic and another thing entirely to use it to advance your spiritual journey. So, it would be in your best interests to decide now that this will be the start of a long and very fruitful endeavor for you. This book has been written to simplify what Enochian magic is so that you can confidently take the next step of applying it in your life.

Chapter 1: Enochian Magic and the Gates of Wisdom

Enochian magic is magic that involves summoning spirits and sending them out to do your will. It's all founded on the teachings of John Dee and Sir Edward Kelley. John Dee was an Anglo-Welsh astronomer, mathematician, alchemist, teacher, astrologer, and occultist. Edward Kelley was also called Edward Kelly or Edward Talbot. He was an English occultist and spirit medium from the Renaissance period who could summon spirits using a mirror or *shew stone* (a stone gazed into to see or predict the future).

These two men claim that they received all Enochian information and the language directly from different angels, all called the Enochian angels. In Dee's journals, you'll find the Enochian script, an angelic occult language. These men had visions that gave them all the secrets from the Book of Enoch, Hebrew text from ancient times attributed to Enoch.

The Enochian magic system is based on various channelings or communication with angels from 1582 to 1589. Dee got his information from angels. On the other hand, Kelley was into scrying (seeing the future using a crystal ball or other reflective object). While the former had well-kept records, Kelley would look into a shew stone of crystal and narrate all he could see.

There are two kinds of Enochian magic practitioners. You have the Enochian magicians influenced by the teachings of Aleister

Crowley and the Hermetic Order of the Golden Dawn and those who consider themselves **Dee Purists,** who follow the work of Dee as it was written.

The Men Behind the Magic

Dee intended to use the magic taught to him by the angels to help Queen Elizabeth I with her expansionist ideas and decrees when Spain was dangerously close to invading England. He wanted to keep all of Europe's rulers in check by working with the guardian spirits of each nation. Dee was a great cartographer, astronomer, and mathematician. Some claim that he was also the private counselor, astrologer, and espionage agent of Her Majesty the Queen Elizabeth the First. He was always loyal to her cause, and he was well known for his magical skills all over Europe.

Kelley was a man who had always wanted to find the truth of the philosopher's stone and had considerable experience in necromancy, a dark art. Accused of forging title deeds in 1580, he had to flee Lancaster. So, he set out to tour Wales. Legend has it that when he got close to Glastonbury, he bought a bit of the red powder that's said to convert base metals into pure gold from an innkeeper who got it from tomb raiders.

Kelley then spent the rest of his life working to unlock the power of the red powder so that he could create more of it. As he sought this knowledge, he came upon John Dee's library in 1582, and that's why he chose to work as a seer for Dee. It was an odd pairing since most would describe Dee as a saint and Kelley as a sinner, yet they had a common interest in ceremonial magic and its potentials. Dee didn't have much skill with mediumship, a problem he tried to work around by getting a professional scryer, but that didn't work out. So, when he'd heard about Kelley's abilities with psychic work, he promptly employed the man.

Dee would summon the Enochian angels into the physical world close to a black obsidian mirror or a scrying crystal using magical seals and prayers. Then, when Kelley saw the angels had arrived, Dee would ask them questions. Kelley would then tell him their answers, and Dee would, in turn, write them down in his diaries.

The most significant part of Dee's work was *A True and Faithful Relation of What Passed for Many Years between Dr. John Dee...*

and Some Spirits. Meric Casaubon published this in 1659 in London, and it's been reprinted a considerable number of times since then.

The Enochian spirits are named for the nature of the system of magic they talk about. They claim that this is the same magic that Enoch had mastered from the angels of heaven. Ave, one of the angels, said to Dee that it was God's will to give this same doctrine once again to Dee. It's nothing like any other form of magic you know.

While Dee was diligent about writing the magic down in his diaries, he didn't take it seriously enough to make it work for him, and it's not clear why. In 1589, he and Kelley parted ways, the latter remaining in Bohemia to create gold on behalf of Rudolph II, the Holy Roman Emperor. Dee chose to head back to England at the queen's request, and this may have played some part in keeping him from magical practice, according to some. Others theorize that he had waited for the angels to permit him to use the magic, but that permission never came in this life.

Dee was a renaissance philosopher in that he was all about connecting with the divine to understand nature's law. For him, there were three "books" through which God gave all his secrets: nature, the human soul, and the revealed scripture. For Dee, math underlies every part of natural philosophy. He also believed that there were three states of numbers. First, there's the "Numbers numbering," which is God the creator of all; the "Numbers numbered," which is every creature that is bound to deteriorate with time; and "Intermediaries" that stood between the first two-state, which is the mind of man and angels.

Just Two Mad Men Forging a New Religion?

It's very easy to assume — especially if you haven't the foggiest idea what Enochian magic is all about — that Kelley and Dee had simply faked their communications with angels. They both believed one hundred percent that the angels were real, but they shared different ideas about their motives. While Dee thought they were God's agents who obeyed Christ, Kelley didn't trust them one bit and thought they were deceitful in some way. The angels, not being pushovers, were amused by Kelley's view on them and held some contempt for him. He bore their insults for so long only because he had hoped they would one day tell him the secret of the gold-making red powder.

These angels were clearly intelligent and independent beings who had their own personalities and motives. This envisioning is how Dee and Kelley saw them, and for the would-be Enochian magician, this is the best way to think of them as well.

Enochian Magic Simplified

This form of magic is reminiscent of the kind found within JK Rowling's books – you have to chant something to make something happen. Enochian magic is ceremonial, making use of rituals like casting circles and drawing triangles. You also can use a rounded mirror or crystal to communicate with the angels or spirits, a practice of divination known as *scrying*. For this to work, the surface you use must be reflective so that you can see the spirits when you're in an altered state of consciousness during your rituals.

Four main themes were born of Dee's conversations with the angels. First, there were talks about cosmic order and how essential the angels are to sustaining it. Secondly, there were details about magical invocations and rituals. Third, they spoke of prophecies and apocalyptic predictions, foretelling the beginning and end of empires, which was connected to the level of spiritual piety. Finally, there was the *Lingua Adamica,* which was the Enochian language itself. In this language are specific pentacles and sigils that Kelley and Dee used as well. Sigils (written or painted symbols thought to have magical power) are a vital part of Enochian magic. After Dee and Kelley, they were repurposed in Celtic magic and other magic forms in a personalized way.

Enochian Mythology

God created the world with a set of divine words written in fiery letters on several heavenly tablets collectively called the *Book of the Speech from God.* This book has the heavenly creation language, the keys to the heavenly gates, and all wisdom and knowledge of the entire universe, from the past, present, and the future. It shows up in so many religions in different ways, referred to as the *Book of Life, the Book of Thoth, the Tablets of Destiny, the Heavenly Tablets, the Book of the Lamb, the Book of the Secrets of God, Book T (T for Tarot)*, and *the Akashic Records.*

In the garden of Eden – paradise on Earth – it was the celestial language that Adam used to speak to God and his angels. It was the same language he used to name all the animals. However, Adam fell from grace when he disobeyed God, and so he lost all he knew about the sacred tongue. He could no longer remain in touch with the angels. He developed the human language to communicate with his family, founded on what flawed, incomplete fragments he could recall of celestial speech.

Seven generations passed, and Enoch (the prophet) found a way to connect with the angels like Adam used to. The angels believed he was worthy enough to see the heavens, God's throne, the choir of angels, and the celestial tablets. From these tablets, the prophet was able to transcribe 366 books full of the wisdom of the ages, which he intended to use to restore humankind to its former glory. However, everything Enoch had written down was lost in the Great Flood.

Adam's language was passed down through Noah's bloodline until the event at the Tower of Babel, where there was a confusion of languages. God had made it so the people could no longer understand one another; he did this by giving them different languages. The one language closest to Adam's primordial one that we still have is Biblical Hebrew. Many have since then tried to recreate the language of heaven, but they usually just produce languages that are copycats of the Biblical Hebrew language – mere shadows of the true language of the divine.

By the 1500s, Dee and Kelley became interested in the lost language. They used the grimoires of Solomon to reach out to the angels who had spoken to Enoch a long time ago. Those angels shared many secrets of magic with them, like how to summon divine beings of the stars and planets, know what other nations are hiding, and how to visit the heavens.

Dee had requested that these divine beings reveal the Book of Enoch to him, which was on the prophet's work and life. The angels acquiesced, but instead, they showed him the Book of the Speech from God, which Enoch copied from the Celestial Tablets. This volume is now known as the Ethiopic Book of Enoch or 1 Enoch, which you can find online, free of charge. It's described as a large tome with all 49 pages written in the blood of the Lamb, having 49 divine speeches that God created the world with. The angels showed Kelley and Dee how to open heaven's gates with this book to get revelations from God himself – and commune with the angels. Dee never referred to his magic system by what it's known as today; it was given the term "Enochian magic" by historians much later. This magic is also heavily inspired by the Kabbalistic Gates of Binah (or wisdom).

De Heptarchia Mystica

This book is also called *On the Mystical Rule of the Seven Planets.* It was written circa 1582 by John Dee and provided guidance to the reader on how to summon angels under angel Uriel's guidance. Also known simply as The Heptarchia, meaning seven-fold rulership, it's the name of the Enochian planetary angel magic system. In their journals, Kelley and Dee spelled out the names of every Heptarchic angel, what they look like, what they do, and the sigils they have.

The Angelic Calls

These are also known as the Enochian Calls or Keys. They are the magical incantations Dee and Kelley used to call upon the angels and elementary sports. These 19 calls are written in the Enochian language, and they have a remarkable consistency in syntax and grammar. The first two are used to summon spirits, while six are for summoning the elements of air, fire, water, and earth. The 19th key is for summoning whichever of the 30 Aethyrs you desire. Kelley had to dictate the calls backward because doing them correctly (forward) would summon forces too powerful to contain.

Aleister Crowley and Victor Neuburg had once worked some magical operations with these Enochian Keys. In the middle of the process, Crowley came upon some principles which he honed into a sex magic system, and he wrote about this in a long article he published in the Equinox (and later in a book titled <u>The Vision and the Voice</u>.) Crowley's writings made Enochian magic very popular to magicians of the twentieth century; he then went on to develop this as a form of ceremonial magic. Others who have used Enochian magic include Anton LaVey, who adapted it to work with his Satanic system, which he wrote about in his book, *The Satanic Bible.*

The Enochian Map

Dee drew a map of the universe as a square with four elemental watchtowers or tablets, which had the Tablet of Union, with 30 concentric circles – also called the 30 airs or aethyrs. These are numbered from the 30th on (TEX), the lowest one closest to the watchtowers, and to the first (LIL) – the one that's the highest and represents Supreme Attainment. Enochian magicians wrote their visions and impressions of each aethyr (heaven), which has three governors, except for the lowest one, which has four. In total, there are 91 governors, each of them with their sigil that you can trace on the Great Tablet of Earth. When it comes to practical Enochian magic, the 19th Call of the 30 aethyrs is used only when working with the aethyrs.

The angels of the four quarters are represented by the Elemental watchtowers, also known as the Great Table of the Earth. Many of the popular Enochian angels are pulled from the watchtowers of this great table.

Each of the watchtowers represents a classical element which is subsequently ruled by order of spiritual entities in this hierarchy:

- The Three Holy Names
- The Great Elemental King
- The Six Elders
- The Two Divine Names on the Cross of Calvary
- The Kerubim
- The 16 Lesser Angels

Every watchtower is split further into four groups, also called sub-quadrants, where the names of the archangels and angels who rule these worlds are written. So, the entire universe, seen and unseen, is shown as brimming with all sorts of intelligence. The elemental tablets are also split into four by the Great Central Cross, which has two vertical columns in the center called the *Linea Filli* and the *Linea Patris*. A horizontal line runs through the center called the *Linea Spiritus Sancti*.

Besides the four elemental watchtowers, there is a cell with 21 squares called the Tablet of Union or the Black Cross. This cell represents the spirit and forms the complete picture of the five elemental attributes of Spirit, Water, Fire, Air, and Earth. These squares are more like truncated pyramids (they have flat tops), giving them five sides in total, representing the elements.

The Tablet of Union has 20 pyramids and 156 in each of the Elemental Tablets. The pyramids each have an angel with a name made up of just one letter. The nature and powers of the angels can be deduced from where it is positioned in the Tablet and the proportions of the various elements that its sides show. When you combine two pyramids, you get an angel that has a name with two letters and more complex attributes. Following this logic, you can create more and more complex angels depending on the number of pyramids you work with.

Is Enochian Magic Evil?

There are way too many misconceptions and lies about this magic system that are being paraded as truth to dissuade you from practicing it. Some think that this magic is pure evil because of how chaotic and complex it appears, but that couldn't be further from the truth. The truth is that this magic system is powerful. Taking the time to learn and practice it will unlock a door to a wonderful world of mysticism for you.

Manuscripts

While most Enochian magicians accept that Dee and Kelley received all their information from scrying and communing with angels, the material they produce shares some similarities to grimoires like the *Heptameron*. It was written by Pietro d'Abano (also called Peter of Abano, Petrus Aponensis, or Petrus de Apono), an Italian professor of medicine, philosopher, and astrologer from Padua. Dee was familiar with Pietro's work before he and Kelley divined the message from the angels. Some of the messages are also reminiscent of the magical works by Reuchlin,

Agrippa, and the *Book of Soyga.*

The Liber Loagaeth (also known as the *Book of Enoch; Liber Mysteriorum, Sextus et Sanctus (The Sixth and Sacred Book of the Mysteries; and the Book of the Speech of God)* is another important manuscript in Enochian magic. You might see it spelled as Logaeth, but that's just a misspelling that happened so often it became accepted. To be clear, The Book of Enoch shouldn't be mistaken for The Book of Enoch in the Bible, which has three versions, nor Aleister Crowley's own *Liber Chanokh.*

This book has 73 folios and was written by Edward Kelley. It has 96 magical grids made up of very complex letters. Ninety-four of these grids are 49 by 49 grids of magical letters, and one of them is a table with 49 rows of texts, while another has 9 rows of letters in addition to 40 rows of text. The last folio has 21 words which have 112 letters. The text claims that it's possible to reduce them all to 105 letters that you can then arrange into five tables of 3 by 7, with two on the back and three on the front. The Liber Loagaeth is where Kelley and Dee got the 48 Keys or Calls, which have hidden within them the keys that grant you access to the *Mystical Heptarchy.*

Another vital manuscript is *Mysteriorum Libri Quinque* or *Five Books of Mystery.* This manuscript talks about the following:

- The temple's furniture
- The *Sigillum Dei Aemeth* or Seal of God
- The Great Circle
- The Collected Table of 49 Good Angels
- The Tables of Light
- The Tables of Creation
- Dee's copies of the Angelic Alphabet
- The start of the Loagaeth

Other manuscripts include:

- MS Cotton Appendix XLVI Part I
- MS Cotton Appendix XLVI Part II

Chapter 2: John Dee — Elizabethan Mystic or Polymath?

A Biography of John Dee

Dee was born July 13, 1527, in Tower Ward, London, England. He died on March 26, 1609, in Mortlake, London, England. As an English scholar, he wrote on calendar reform, trigonometry, astrology, geography, and navigation. He became an astrologer to Her Majesty Queen Mary, but then he was thrown into prison for working magic.

His father, Roland Dee, was of Welsh descent. He was in the business of textiles and worked in Henry VIII's court as a gentleman sewer. John's mother was named Jane Wild, and she married Roland when she was only 15. At the age of 18, she had their first and only child, John.

Education

John studied at a Chelmsford school in Essex from 1535. In November 1542, he entered St. John's College, Cambridge. There, he learned philosophy, Latin, Greek, astronomy, arithmetic, and geometry. He was so bent on learning that he would work for 18 hours every day, sleeping only four hours and saving two hours for his meals. In 1546, he started making astronomical observations. While he was a proponent of astrology, just like most others of his day, he wanted a scientific reason why the planets' placements affect our lives. To him, every heavenly body had a ray of force that affected every other body. He primarily used mathematics as the vehicle to reach his answers.

In 1546, he graduated, becoming a Fellow of St. John's College. Come December of that same year, he became a Fellow of Trinity College, Cambridge, founded by Henry VIII. (Of all the Cambridge colleges, Trinity is the largest.)

Travel

John Dee wasn't happy with the way science was approached in England, so he traveled around from 1548 to 1551. He first went to Louvain, close to Brussels, arriving on 24 June 1548. There, he studied alongside Gerardus Mercator and Gemma Frisius. With time, Mercator and Dee grew close and would talk about novel models for explaining the universe. In Louvain, Dee penned two works on astronomy. By 1550, he moved on to Brussels, engaging with the mathematicians there. In Brussels, he met Pedro Nunez, a Portuguese scholar, and became good friends with him. Many loved Dee's lectures and would flock to hear him speak in overpacked lecture rooms. In 1551, Dee declined an appointment he was offered in Paris to become a professor of mathematics and an Oxford lectureship in mathematics three years later.

Back to England, John served the Earl of Pembroke in 1552, then moved on to serve the Duke of Northumberland towards the end of that year, which is when he wrote about tides. When King Edward VI died, there was a lot of bad blood between the Protestants and Catholics, creating much confusion regarding who should succeed the late king. Against the desires of the Protestants, Catholic Queen Mary rose to power, and she then began a campaign against Protestants of significant status. One of the people arrested in August 1553 was John Dee's father; he was eventually released after all his financial assets had been stripped from him. If this hadn't happened, John would have inherited a good share of wealth from his father, allowing him to further his studies without worrying about making ends meet.

Trouble

On May 28, 1555, John Dee was also arrested, accused of "calculating." It sounds ludicrous now, but in England in those days, mathematics was thought of as having magical powers, which the Catholic Church clearly opposed. In fact, mathematical books were burned as though they were books for conjuring entities. John Dee was not just some mystic or a mad magician; he was a polymath who had a deep love for learning. He was held for three months and then released, but not without them taking away his income sources and causing him financial difficulties. His father died in 1555 without reclaiming his wealth.

Dee did his best not to side with Protestants or Catholics, but after he was released, he seemed to have made peace with the Catholic crown — the same one that threw him in prison and ruined his father financially. He may have made himself at home with the enemy as a matter of political convenience, but there's also a chance he was acting as a spy.

A New Alliance

On January 15, 1556, he presented his plan to Queen Mary for a national library, intending to save all the copies of significant books for anyone to learn from. It didn't receive her blessing, but he found a way to set up a library of his own despite financial hardship. In 1558, Queen Mary died, and Elizabeth, a Protestant, took her place as Queen. She favored Dee, and he even picked a good day for her coronation using astrology. Many wondered how he could have gone from being closely connected to the Catholic throne to finding favor with the Protestant Queen so quickly, implying that he might have been spying on the former Queen's administration on behalf of Elizabeth.

A Brilliant Scholar and Scientist

For the next five years, Dee would travel abroad seeking books to fill his library and satisfy his thirst for knowledge in coding, astrology, mathematics, astronomy, and magical matters, which, in his mind, were all connected. He felt that finding the common thread running through all these studies would help him find the ultimate truth about life. Although Dee was close to the new Queen and would often advise her, he still never got the money needed to focus completely on studying. He lived with his mother in 1566 at Mortlake, London, to reduce his expenses. He collected an impressive amount of scholarly material and globes, astronomical instruments, and accurate clocks.

He published *Propaedeumata Aphoristica* in 1568 and presented the publication to Queen Elizabeth. She was so impressed that she had Dee teach her mathematics to better understand the book, which had a lot of magic, astrology, mathematics, and physics. If you feel reluctant to consider this man a genius because of his love for magic, understand that the greatest mathematicians and scientists of that time and even later had the same interests. Kepler, Cavalieri, and Brahe believed firmly in astrology –. Newton was absolutely taken with alchemy, just like Dee. So, you see, Dee was a brilliant scientist. He had written in *Propaedeumata Aphoristica* that all objects of unequal masses would fall at the same velocity, and he had referred to scientists before him who made this fact clear. He also stated that all objects in the universe exert some force on every other object.

Dee had edited one of Euclid's Elements editions in 1570, as translated by Billingsley. He wrote a very famous preface where he argued for the study of mathematics. He observed Tycho Brahe's 1572 supernova, and the year after that, he wrote about triogonomics in *Parallacticae Commentationis Praxosque.* In it, he talked about the various methods of trigonometry which you could use to calculate the distance between Earth and Brahe's new star. Along with Thomas Digges (his assistant), he accurately observed the star, and they were in touch with Brahe about it.

Dee returned in 1551 from the Continent with navigation instruments. He consulted for the Muscovy Company in 1555, the same year the company was formed by Sebastian Cabot, an explorer and navigator, and a bunch of merchants from London. It was given a monopoly of trade between England and Russia, and one of its goals was to find the Northeast Passage. It was Dee who prepared all the charts for navigation in polar areas and other nautical information on behalf of the company for the next 32 years. He was the one who taught the crew about cosmography and geometry before they took off for North America in 1576.

In February 1578, Dee married his third wife, Jane Fromands, and they had eight children. (His second wife died in March 1576, and they had no children, just like his first marriage.) By 1579, his mother, Jane, let him have her Mortlake house, where he had lived for at least 13 years. His mother died in By 1580.

In February 1583, Dee had proposed to Queen Elizabeth that the calendar should be reformed. He wanted to get rid of 11 days to coordinate the calendar with the astronomical year. This was the right thing to do, and he received support from some of Elizabeth's advisors. However, the Archbishop of Canterbury didn't like the scheme because he'd been in a long-time disagreement with Her Majesty – and also because he thought it resembled the same thing the Catholic Church had done the year before. Yet, it was hard to deny that Dee's plan was better than the calendar proclaimed to all by Pope Gregory XIII, founded on the Council of Nicaea in 325. So, until 1752, England's calendar remained different from all of the rest of Europe!

Dee Meets Kelley

In March 1582, Dee met Edward Kelley, a medium with the skills to reach out to spirits and angels by gazing into a reflective surface like a crystal ball. This, however, wasn't Dee's first rodeo with practices like these. In the beginning, he was very mistrustful of the validity of Kelley's visions, but with time, he came to realize that Kelley had remarkable skill in his trade, and he also was desperate to understand life's ultimate truth. He had tried every other method known to man at the time and had failed, and it also didn't help that many did not react well to his scientific findings.

Visions in Crystal

Dee was involved in crystallomancy. As he lived mostly on his own, doing astrology to keep his head afloat and studying alchemy (his true love), he would pore over mysteries of the Talmud and Rosicrucian ideologies. He was taken by ideas of the philosopher's stone and the elixir of life, and at some point, he began to have visions that convinced him he should look into the world unseen some more. The very first time he saw spirits, according to his *Diary,* was on May 25, 1581.

In November 1582, Dee was in deep, fervent prayer when he suddenly noticed that there was a glorious sight that took up his lab's west window. It was none other than the angel Uriel himself. Dee was stunned by the angel's glory. Uriel smiled, handed him a piece of crystal — a convex one — and then told him all he had to do to reach out to beings from a world besides ours was to look deeply into the crystal, and they would come through and tell him all the mysteries of life and the future. Then Uriel disappeared.

Dee did as he was instructed but found he had to concentrate very hard before the spirits would show up, let alone answer him. He also found it hard to recall what they would tell him each time they spoke. So, he needed someone to work with him to speak with the spirits while noting what they said. Some believe that Kelley duped Dee, who was so desperate to unravel life's mysteries that he would have believed anything Kelley said; that's a different matter that we won't cover here.

Dee engaged in more and more conversations with spirits and angels through Kelley, which took about five years. Both men visited Bohemia and Poland from 1583 to 1589, displaying magic at various courts. Kelley became wealthy and famous and was eventually knighted, while Dee remained financially troubled. In December 1589, he went back to Mortlake only to find that his library was missing many books and scientific instruments. This was the same period he and Thomas Harriot became good friends.

Dee did his best for years to be compensated for the lost income since his imprisonment. He attempted to get appointed as Master of St. John's Cross, which Queen Elizabeth approved. All that was needed was the approval of the Canterbury Archbishop, but that never happened, so he was unable to seal the deal. By 1596, he became the warden of the Collegiate Chapter in Manchester, which is speculated was a ploy to get him out of London. Manchester then suffered a deadly plague in 1605, and there Dee lost his wife and some of his children. He eventually went back to London and died just a few years later.

Chapter 3: Unlocking the Secrets of the Book of Enoch

The Book of Enoch has over 100 chapters and was based on an obscure Biblical character called Enoch. In the Bible, Enoch shows up briefly in Adam's genealogy after fathering Methuselah and other children. In Genesis Chapter 5 verse 24, the Bible says: "Enoch walked with God; then he was no more because God took him." That's a pretty cryptic verse. Early Christians and Jews weren't okay with that vagueness, so the Book of Enoch was born as a spinoff. It was very popular, so much so that it is referred to in the New Testament.

Considering how popular the book was for Ancient Jews and Christians, it's a little too obscure in our times.

What Is the Book of Enoch?

There is more than one book, but when people say, "The Book of Enoch," they typically mean the first book, 1 Enoch. There's a second and a third Enoch as well. We'll focus on the first one. Another thing to remember is that this is not a book as much as a combination of many connected texts. You can distinguish this by the abrupt changes between its parts; it's almost as if someone just compiled many separate works.

There are five main sections and two appendices. The main sections are:

- Book of the Watchers (Chapters 1 to 36)
- Book of Parables (Chapters 37 to 71)
- Book of the Luminaries (Chapters 72 to 82)
- The Dream Visions (Chapters 83 to 90)
- The Epistle of Enoch (Chapters 91 to 105)

The two appendices are:

- The Birth of Noah (Chapters 106 to 107)
- The Final Book of Enoch (Chapter 108)

The oldest parts are likely from the 4th or 3rd century BCE. The most complete manuscripts are from around the 15th or 16th centuries and are written in Ethiopic. This language is also called Ge'ez – a cousin of Arabic, Amharic, and Hebrew, being a Semitic language itself. It is the Ethiopic Orthodox Church's liturgical language, much like Latin is for the Roman Catholic Church's liturgies or Coptic for Coptic Orthodox Christians.

The Book of Enoch journeyed long, from when it was composed to when we got the fullest version of the manuscripts. Enoch was most likely written in Aramaic first before it was translated to Greek and then Ethiopic. At the site of Qumran, there were many Aramaic versions of the Book of Enoch's Aramaic among the Dead Sea scrolls. In a single tablet of the Dead Sea Scroll, you'll find several sections of Enoch's texts, making it clear that all the various sections were already popular, moving around as a single compilation by the 1st century.

In total, there are 90 manuscripts of this book in various forms. That being said, some of them have remarkable differences, especially when compared to previous versions. It's why you need to find a good version that will account for these differences if you're going to read it on your own. A good one is the Hermeneia Translation, published by Fortress Press, written by George Nickelsburg and James VanderKam.

The Book of the Watchers

This section is the first part of 1st Enoch. It shares some stories with the Hebrew Bible, like those of Adam and Eve, their children Cain and Abel, and how God's sons or angels married human women. However, some differences make the Book of Enoch fascinating, like the fall of angels gone rogue.

The book develops two intriguing snatches from Genesis into an entire book filled with fascinating visions and stories. We've already seen the first blurb, which consists of a few brief phrases stating that God took Enoch. The second snippet, which serves as the inspiration for the entire opening scene of 1st Enoch, is a strange narrative from Genesis Chapter 6, verses 1 to 4, about supernatural entities having sexual relations with humans. According to Genesis, before Noah's deluge, divine beings are known as the "Children of God" descended to earth to have intercourse with human women, who then bore the Nephilim.

According to the scripture, these Nephilim were legendary warriors from ancient times. Other than that, there is no more indication of who the Nephilim were or their accomplishments. There is no backstory for these divine sons, which suggests one thing: it's the type of story that begs for continuation. In the Book of the Watchers, Enoch substantially expands on these few verses. God's sons are no longer a nebulous group of heavenly creatures but instead a collection of fallen angels known as The Watchers.

Shemihaza, their Chief, commands them. Their descendants, the Nephilim, are colossal beings who began wreaking havoc on the planet. According to Enoch Chapter 7, verse 3, the giants began murdering and devouring men and then slaughtering and devouring all beasts. Additionally, this part identifies The Watchers as cunning angels who were adept at teaching humanity wicked supernatural arts. The Watcher Asael, according to Chapter 8, taught humanity how to use weapons of war. They learned sorcery from Shemihaza. Others demonstrated astrology to humans.

As The Watchers and Giants continue to ruin the Earth and corrupt humans with bad knowledge, the story culminates with humanity calling out to God for assistance. God responds by sending four archangels to correct what was done. He directs one to warn Noah of the flood to come, while another is to confine and send the fallen angel Isaiah into darkness. God directs Gabriel to eliminate the Nephilim in a horrifying chapter, instructing him to go to the "bastards" and "half-breeds" and destroy them.

Finally, God assigns archangel Michael the job of imprisoning Shemihaza, the king of The Watchers. God sends Enoch to The Watchers to warn them of their impending destruction. The remainder of Enoch is primarily prophecy and visions. The overarching themes that run through these predictions are the hope for a Messiah, the last judgment, salvation, the resurrection, and journeys through the heavens. All of them are defining characteristics of 1st Enoch's cultural setting and genre.

Similarities to the Book of Daniel

Apocalyptic literature, or *Jewish apocalypticism*, is the term scholars use to refer to a collection of works that grew extremely popular during the second temple period. These were scriptures that described visions of paradise in which an angel revealed the end times or the impending judgment of the world to a prophet. Enoch is one of the earliest Jewish apocalyptic scriptures, dating back even further than another well-known apocalyptic text called the Book of Daniel.

If we accept the agreement that Daniel was authored in the Hellenistic period of the second century BCE, phrases popularly associated with Daniel such as "Son of Man" and "Messiah" originate in the book of Enoch. Enoch has a vision of the commissioning of the Son of Man in one chapter. It tells us that he will be the righteous man's staff, lighting up nations, and every living soul will prostrate themselves before him. If you know your New Testament, this type of phrase should sound familiar as it is also applied to Jesus.

However, Enoch is dubbed the Son of Man in this passage. "You are that Son of Man who was born for righteousness" (Chapter 71 verse 14). Additionally, The Book of Enoch contains the concept of hell, another later Christian theological concept. The concept of hell is not found in the earlier Hebrew Bible texts; it is a later addition that acquired prominence during the second temple period, particularly in apocalyptic literature.

Enoch sees a tiny fissure reaching the abyss in Chapter 21, verse 7, when he witnesses a tremendous fire raging. It is written, "This is a prison for the angels. Here they will be confined forever." Essentially, the entire text of Enoch is concerned with the notion that the current world is bad and requires judgment and renewal. We are approaching a new era. God's ultimate wrath is upon us. However, what happened to it in the subsequent years? 1st Enoch had a tremendous influence on subsequent generations of Christians, Jews, and even Muslims. Let us begin with a brief history of the practice within Judaism. 1st Enoch influenced several Jewish works that are not canonical. Indeed, another second temple Jewish literature called *Jubilees,* preserved in Ethiopic and discovered in Hebrew at Qumran, parallels Enoch in numerous ways. While the Book of Enoch was a significant part of the Judaism of the second temple, it has little importance in current Judaism.

Rabbinic Judaism's Stance on Enoch

Rabbinic Judaism refuted two major statements made in the Enoch-related literature. First, they refuted the belief that Enoch never saw death and that rebellious angels visited the earth during the flood. As a result, Enoch does not appear in the Hebrew Bible's canonical books and only occasionally in rabbinic literature, and when he does, it is in a negative light. 3rd Enoch is a significant exception to the generally negative view of Enoch in rabbinic literature. It tells the tale of Enoch becoming the angel Metatron. Here, he is called a *lesser Yahweh* once he has transfigured.

While other mystical rabbinic works reference Enoch, Rabbinic Judaism does not regard them as authoritative. Surprisingly, Kabbalistic works like the Zohar praise Enoch and relate him to Adam and make references to the Book of Enoch to clarify problematic biblical phrases. Annette Reed, a scholar of late Christianity and Judaism, thinks that this is a product of the ongoing cross-cultural exchange between Jews and Christians throughout late antiquity because Christians appeared to really like this work, at least initially.

The New Testament's Book of Jude makes a direct reference to 1st Enoch. Also, Enoch almost certainly influenced the gospels' and Book of Revelation's theology. For example, the concept of the Son of Man, which appears in Mark's Gospel, bears theological resemblance to 1st Enoch. The Book of Revelation resembles the Book of the Parables' apocalypse as both describe a throne chamber coupled with ultimate judgment.

Initially, Christians considered 1st Enoch to be significant. Church fathers such as Justin Martyr and Irenaeus referenced and utilized the book. Even Chartullian maintains the book's authority, and the Epistle of Barnabas — which is non-canonical — refers to it as scripture. Enoch, however, appeared to have fallen out of popularity by the 4th century. By the 7th and 8th centuries, prominent church fathers such as Augustine and Jerome had already condemned it. 1st Enoch retained popularity solely in Ethiopia, which is still included in the Ethiopian Orthodox Church's Biblical canon. Ethiopian Christianity has a significantly larger Biblical canon than Christianity's other branches, consisting of over 81 books. By incorporating Enoch, the book has left an indelible mark on Ethiopian Christians.

The Second Book of Enoch

2nd Enoch talks about the *Grigori,* much likened to the same beings as The Watchers. They are innumerable soldiers who look human but are greater in size than the greatest of giants. They have their home in the fifth heaven, and they, along with Satanail, their prince, revolted against God. One of the versions of 2nd Enoch says that they were 200 myriads — in modern-day English, 2 million. Just like in the first book of Enoch, they went down from Heaven to Earth and married human women, and this led to them being imprisoned underground.

Before humans were created — on the second day, to be precise — it is written that one from the archangels' order had an "impossible thought." He had wanted to set his throne as high as the Lord God so that they could be of the same standing. For this reason, God banished him from Heaven along with his angels, and he continued to move around in the air "above the bottomless."

According to the *Mercer Dictionary of the Bible,* there's a difference between the fallen angels and the Grigori, as in the fifth heaven, Enoch gets to see giants who were brothers of the now fallen beings.

Chapter 4: Nephilim — The Fallen Angels

In the Hebrew Bible, the Nephilim are a group of mysterious, spiritual beings who are incredibly large and strong, existing before and after the Great Flood. They are referred to in the books of Genesis and Numbers, and arguably, Ezekiel. The word Nephilim is from the Hebrew *nefilim,* which is sometimes translated as "giants" and other times refers to "the fallen ones," thanks to the Hebrew word for the phrase "to fall," *naphal.* However, there's some debate among scholars about who these beings are.

What the Scriptures Say

In Genesis Chapter 6 verse 4, right before the account of the Great Flood, it is written, "*The Nephilim were on the earth in those days — and also afterward — when the sons of God went into the daughters of humans, who bore children to them. These were the heroes that were of old, warriors of renown.*"

The book of Numbers, Chapter 13, verses 32 to 33, also mentions these beings as the people of God (the Israelites) were getting ready to head into Canaan. It says:

"So they brought the Israelites an unfavorable report of the land that they had spied out, saying, '*The land that we have gone through as spies is a land that devours its inhabitants, and all the people that we saw in it are of great size. There we saw the Nephilim (the Anakites come from the Nephilim), and to ourselves, we seemed like grasshoppers, and so we seemed to them.' "*

Scholars debate that the "fallen mighty men" spoken of in the book of Ezekiel Chapter 32 verse 27 is talking about the Nephilim indirectly, as the Hebrew phrase is a bit vague. This passage talks about the states and the pit of the grave, saying:

"And they do not lie with the fallen warriors of long ago who went down to Sheol with their weapons of war, whose swords were laid under their heads, and whose shields are upon their bones; for the terror of the warriors was in the land of the living."

Since the passage in Genesis is too vague, there are many interpretations of the connection between the Nephilim and the sons of God. One school of thought holds that the sons of God are the same as the fallen angels and that the Nephilim are the children they had with human women. This view was given by 1st Enoch and is a very popular one. Also, in the Book of Enoch, it is stated that the Nephilim were giants, and that fact lines up nicely with the phrase "people of great size" that we find in the passage from the book of Numbers. It is argued that the Nephilim received their giant traits from supernatural sources, but some argue that the flaw in this logic is that demons and angels are entirely spiritual, and therefore do not have the capacity to mate with humans, let alone reproduce.

Another school of thought believes that the Nephilim are just regular people who stopped following the path of righteousness. They believe that the phrase "sons of God" refers to Seth's descendants — Seth being Adam's remaining righteous son. Proponents of this view believe that the Nephilim are people of the bloodline that turned their backs on God. This is also called the Sethian view, and Saint Augustine and other Church Fathers believed this firmly. The Sethian view also holds that "daughters of men" refers to the women from Cain's bloodline, who were ungodly. Remember, Cain was the first murderer on earth. They consider the phrase "great size" as more of a metaphor, or even if literally, they don't think of these Nephilim as giants in that sense of the word. They do, however, allow that these beings were warriors in their own right.

Further Analysis of the Book of Enoch

The Great Flood is a story that begins towards the end of the *Parashat Bereshit* and continues in *Parashat Noah*. In the book of Genesis, Chapter 6, verses 5 and 6, it is written:

"And the Lord saw that the wickedness of man was great on the earth and that the inclination of the thoughts of his heart was only evil continually. And the Lord regretted that He had made man on the earth, and it grieved his heart."

Nothing in the Torah specifically talks about this wickedness, but interpretation from early Judaism helps us fill in the blanks. *The Book of the Watchers* addresses the origin of evil. The word "Watchers" is derived from the Aramaic term that means "the awake ones" and can be found in the book of Daniel Chapter 4 verses 10, 14, and 30. These are angels who never sleep, and they show up as *benei ha-elohim* (meaning "sons of God") in Genesis Chapter 6 verses 1 to 4, right after the flood, where it's written:

"And it was when men began to multiply on the face of the earth, and daughters were born to them, that the benei ha-elohim saw the daughters of men that they were fair, and they took wives from whomever they chose. And God said: 'My spirit shall not abide in man forever, for that he also is flesh, and his days be a hundred and twenty years.' The Nephilim were on the earth in those days, and also after that when the benei ha-elohim came to the daughters of men, and they bore children to them; these were the mighty men that were of old, the men of renown."

This passage led to a lot of stories about these angels and their sinful acts.

The Watchers' Sin — Three Versions

First, there's the fact that the Watchers taught humans how to fashion weapons for war and makeup for beauty, both of which were deemed forbidden knowledge for humans. According to one account, the angel Asael comes down to earth to teach women how to adorn themselves to encourage lustful thoughts in men and teach men how to make deadly weapons that they could use to go to war with each other. It is written:

"And Asael taught men to make swords, and daggers, and shields and breastplates. And he showed them the things after these, and the art of making them: bracelets, and ornaments, and the art of making up the eyes and of beautifying the eyelids, and the most precious and choice stones, and all [kinds of] colored dyes. And the world was changed. And there was great impiety and much fornication, and they went astray, and all their ways became corrupt."

This forbidden knowledge led to a great amount of sin, which caused God to wipe the earth clean with a flood.

Next, they gave unto man the knowledge of magic and other forbidden things. It is written, "And they taught them charms and spells, and showed them the cutting of roots and trees (medicine)."

Then there's the final sin of having sex with women and babies by them. It is written:

"And it came to pass, when the sons of men had increased, that in those days there were born to them fair and beautiful daughters. And the angels, the sons of heaven, saw them and desired them. And they said to one another: 'Come, let us choose for ourselves wives from the children of men, and let us beget for ourselves children.' And Shemihaza, who was their leader, said to them: 'I fear that you may not wish this deed to be done, and [that] I alone will pay for this great sin.' And they all answered him and said: 'Let us all swear an oath, and bind one another with curses not to alter this plan, but to carry out this plan effectively.' And they (the women) became pregnant and bore large giants, and their height [was] three thousand cubits. These devoured all the toil of men until men were unable to sustain them. And the giants turned against them to devour men. And they began to sin against birds, and against animals, and against reptiles and against fish, and they devoured one another's flesh and drank the blood from it. Then the earth complained about the lawless ones."

Since this union wasn't a natural one, it inevitably led to terrible outcomes. The giants the women bore caused everyone a lot of trouble and caused all the world's creatures to become a part of their violence. In the third version of this tale, the giants were eventually killed, but their spirits were from divine beings who were immortal and therefore couldn't be completely destroyed, but also, they couldn't go to heaven. So, they became the evil spirits that plague the earth, causing moral and physical evil. It is written:

"And now the giants who were born from spirits and flesh will be called evil spirits upon the earth, and on the earth will be their dwelling. And evil spirits came out from their flesh because from above they were created; from the holy Watchers was their origin and first foundation. Evil spirits will be on the earth, and spirits of the evil ones they will be called. And the dwelling of the spirits of heaven is in heaven, but the dwelling of the spirits of earth, who were born on the earth, [is] on earth. And the spirits of the giants... which do wrong and are corrupt, and attack and fight and break on the earth, and cause sorrow, and they eat no food and do not thirst, and are not observed. And these spirits will rise against the sons of men and against the women because they came out [from them]."

If you want more on this story, you can read the Book of Jubilees, and you can find a bit of it in the Qumran incantations and prayers that ridicule the "bastard" spirits. Please note that all the quotations here are taken from *The Ethiopic Book of Enoch: A New Edition in the Light of the Aramaic Dead Sea Fragment* by Michael Knibb.

Were Dee and Kelley Tricked?

Some believe that the truth about Enochian magic is that it was taught to Dee and Kelley by the same fallen spirits of old, masquerading as benevolent. It especially seems plausible when you consider that the events of Genesis Chapter 6 verses 1 through to 4 happened in the same period as when Enoch was alive. This point of view isn't a very popular one, though. If this is true, then you have to think about what the implications might be. According to Dee Purist practitioners of Enochian magic, since Dee and Kelley didn't write a thing about the Nephilim in their diaries and notes, then that means there's nothing to be concerned about.

Another Angle

This tales sounds like a Hollywood story – not to be taken seriously. That said, it's hard to dismiss it because many pagan religions speak about the sons of gods – enough to make you wonder if it's just myth or if there's something more to the matter. If it's not just mythology, then how can consciousness without a body (invisible angels) mate with a physical being and reproduce?

Going through pagan accounts, you can find that many stories show that mortals and immortals coexisted, or at least could bridge the gap between themselves. It's only in our times that we've become dismissive of this idea, except for the story of how Mary, a virgin, became pregnant by the Holy Spirit. How can we dismiss all pagan lore that suggests that gods mated with humans while holding on to the story of Jesus' conception as truth? It's either possible or impossible.

There's also the matter of whether we need to take these stories literally or as metaphors. If we go the literal route, could it be that these gods, angels, or spirits are extraterrestrial? It might seem plausible, but that sort of thinking leads to so many more questions and theories that just don't add up. The best way to look at these myths is from a purely occult angle, doing away with the material and the laws that rule the physical world. What if all of this were purely allegorical?

The first verse of Genesis chapter 6 talks about humankind becoming very populous and having many beautiful daughters. The word *Chalal* means "to profane" or "to be common." These verses could easily imply that humans had profaned the earth by becoming too common, reproducing so fast that there were too many of us. It's also interesting that the verse talks about daughters being born to humans only when we had become too many, but scholars have said this could have just been from another source and therefore out of context.

Verse 2 speaks about the sons of God becoming aware of the beauty of the daughters of men and choosing the ones they would be with. The original translation of that text says nothing about marriage or wives but just a selection of the beautiful ones "so appointed." Also, the process wasn't random, as the word "appointed' comes from the Hebrew word nasim, which implies being given special honor or made superior in some way to others.

Verse 3, again, seems out of context, as it's simply God refusing to allow his spirit to last forever in men, and therefore decided to cap the life of man to 120 years, when before that decision, men lived to be as old as 800 or 900 years, like Methuselah.

The fourth verse talks about the Nephilim existing before and after the Great Deluge, then talks about them having kids by the human women, and those kids were the *haggicorim,* also known as "men of the name' or anshe ha-shem. This means the children were famous, having names to be remembered for always or of great significance. Since we're leaning towards an esoteric angle, we could say that these were sorcerers who knew the secret language of power. They were called "the great ones,' which can easily be interpreted to mean "giants' — and that's just one way to define the word Nephilim.

Nephilim is from the Aramaic and Hebrew root *nphl,* meaning "to fall." So, they could have been normal-sized humans who were "great men" not in the context of being giants but having many achievements, intellectual prowess, or strength in battle, and their fall could be interpreted as spiritual. It's also worth noting that the same sons of God who took human partners taught humanity the sciences of astronomy, writing, adornment, architecture, agriculture, and more, which are all things that have led to our present civilization. They also taught sorcery and magic and were therefore condemned and cursed by Yahweh, according to the book of Enoch. However, one thing to note is that they were not the sons of Yahweh, a bit of the Elohim, and as such, they had no one to answer to but the Semitic Pantheon, Asherah, and El.

Some theologians believe that there's no such thing as fallen angels and that those are simply a metaphor for foreign princes who married commoners not out of duty – but out of lust. They say that these princes had untainted bloodlines, but their lust drove them to dilute their lineage by being with women of lower standing. However, this doesn't ring true, not for the Enochian magician.

To answer our troubling question of how the immortal with no flesh can mate with a human, we have to figure out who a daughter or son of God really is. Could it be an operation of magic that is actually speaking about people who have been consecrated, taken on a godhead, and then had intercourse with another consecrated partner? This is a plausible way to consider things as sex magic has always been part of old pagan religions. The children born of those rituals would naturally be called children of goddesses or gods of that rite. Hebrew religion has ancient pagan roots, so it wouldn't be far-fetched to consider this angle. The giants might have been simple people, men, and women who had sacred parents and, as such, were considered special, consecrated, and even had their own cult following, which means they were famous like their parents.

Gaius Julius Caesar – dubbed the "greatest First Man of Rome" – also included the Goddess Venus in his family lineage. The Julians were revered as "children of the Gods." His great achievements lent further credence to that title. He's not the first great man to have claimed that their bloodline is rooted in divinity. Keeping this framework in mind, you can have a magical child, as it all comes down to highly advanced magic. It's possible to imbue yourself with the glory and attributes of a godhead by identifying with the divinity within you, being of service spiritually, and assuming the godhead yourself.

This implies that there's never been a barrier between humanity and divinity except in the minds of those who believe there's one. In paganism, then and now, it is possible to have a firsthand experience of the gods through chosen surrogates. Therefore, through Enochian magic, you can become a channel for the expression of divinity. There is so much knowledge waiting for you when you begin to communicate with the spirit world. Like John Dee and Edward Kelley, you can also get the knowledge you need about Enochian magic for yourself, learning even that which they didn't get to discover. In this way, you too can become like the giants of the myth. The choice about what to do with the knowledge you get is up to you, whether for good or evil. The door is always open, and all you have to do is walk right through.

Chapter 5: Conversing with Archangels

The Watchers are also called the Seven Archangels, and their job should be to watch over humanity. You can find these mythical entities in the Abrahamic religion upon which Judaism, Islam, and Christianity were founded. In the De Coelesti Hierarchia of Pseudo-Dionysius, which was written sometime in the 4th or 5th century CE, there's a hierarchy of nine levels of the hosts of heaven:

- Angels
- Archangels
- Principalities
- Powers
- Virtues
- Dominions
- Thrones
- Cherubim
- Seraphim

The angels are the lowest, superseded by the archangels. The Judeo-Christian Bible has seven archangels, with Gabriel and Michael being the only ones mentioned by name in the canonical Bible. The other angels were taken out of this Bible in the 4th

---

century at the Council of Rome.

Background

The apocryphal text from Qumran – the Book of Enoch – talks about five other archangels besides Gabriel and Michael. They are Uriel, Raguel, Raphael, Remiel, and Zerachiel. These angels are a part of the fallen angel mythology, an ancient story that existed even before Christ's New Testament. These stories came from the First Temple period (the Bronze Age) in the 10th century BCE when Solomon's temple was built. You can also find tales like these in Hurrian, ancient Greek, and Hellenistic Egypt. The names of these angels are originally from Mesopotamia, a Babylonian civilization.

The myth implies that the fall of man isn't entirely man's own doing but was caused by the fallen angels, along with Asael and their leader Shemihaza. The archangels intervened on behalf of humankind after these angels had done too much damage to Earth.

During the Second Temple period, the myth took another turn. David Suter and other religious scholars said this myth was really about the rules of endogamy – a law about who a high priest of the temple can get married to – in Jewish tradition. Some believe that this story is meant to warn religious leaders not to get married outside of the priesthood and specific families of the community so that his family line can remain pure.

The Fallen Angel in the Book of Revelation

The Protestant Bible and the Catholic church have the battle between Lucifer, a fallen angel, and Michael, an archangel. The battle is documented in the Book of Revelation, not on earth but in heaven. Lucifer wages war against an entire host of angels, but Michael is the only one named among the rest. Pope Damasus and the Council of Rome took out the remaining portions of the story from the canonical Bible.

Michael

Archangel Michael is God's first archangel and the most important one. Micha-el translates to "Who is like God?" which speaks to war between the archangels and fallen angels (caused by Lucifer wanting to be like God). You could, therefore, say that

Michael was the antithesis of Lucifer.

According to the Bible, Michael is the one who advocates on behalf of the people of God (the Israelites) and the *angel general* as well. He showed up in Daniel's visions when he was in the lion's den. It is Michael who leads the armies of God into battle with a great sword against Satan in the Revelation of John. He's also the patron of the Sacrament of the Holy Eucharist. In occult circles, he is linked to the Sun and Sunday.

Gabriel

This archangel is the holy messenger of God. He is also the archangel of revelation, wisdom, visions, and prophecy. His name means, "God has revealed himself mightily," or "hero of God," or "strength of God." He's the one who came to Zacharias, the priest, to let him know that he and his wife would have a son, John the Baptist. He also appeared to Mary, the mother of Jesus, to let her know that she would conceive and bear the Savior of the world, the

Christ. Gabriel is the patron of the Sacrament of Baptism. In occult sects, he is associated with the Moon and Monday.

Raphael

This archangel is not named in the canonical Bible, but it's believed that the Book of John, Chapter 5, verses 2 to 4, are a reference to him that wasn't removed. It is written:

"In [the pond of Bethsaida] lay a great multitude of sick, of blind, of lame, of withered; waiting for the moving of the water. And an angel of the Lord descended at certain times into the pond, and the water was moved. And he that went down first into the pond after the motion of the water was made whole, of whatsoever infirmity he lay under."

Raphael's name means "God's healer" or "God heals." He's the archangel of healing. You can find him in the book of Tobit (an apocryphal book). The patron of the Sacrament of Reconciliation, Raphael, is linked to Mercury and Tuesday in occult sects.

The Rest of the Archangels

These archangels won't be found in the Bible's modern versions, as the Council of Rome of 382 CE deemed the Book of Enoch non-canonical, and so they took it out of the Bible, not deeming them worthy of veneration.

Uriel

Uriel's name means "Fire of God." The archangel of Repentance and the Damned, he was the Watcher meant to look over Hades. Linked to Venus and Wednesday in occult literature, he is the patron of the Sacrament of Confirmation.

Remiel

Also called Jeremiel, Jehudiel, or Jerahmeel, Reniel's name means "Compassion of God," "Mercy of God," or "Thunder of God." He is the archangel of dreams or hope and faith. He's also the patron of the Sacrament of Anointing of the Sick and is linked in occultic literature to Saturn and Thursdays.

Raguel

Also called Sealtiel, Raguel's name means "Friend of God." The patron of the Sacrament of Holy Orders, he is linked to Mars and Friday in occult literature.

Zerachiel

Zerachiel is also called Sariel, Selaphiel, Baruchel, or Saraquel. His name means "God's command." This archangel is in charge of God's Judgment, and he's also the patron of the Sacrament of Matrimony. In occult sects, he is associated with Jupiter and Saturday.

How the Archangels Saved Humanity from the Watchers

You already know that the Watchers, who were supposed to take care of the earth and not interfere in man's affairs, decided to interfere anyway, and as a result, they slept with mortal women and birthed the Nephilim monsters. The Nephilim destroyed homes, fed on the people's animals, crops, the people themselves, and eventually each other. Just as insidious, Azazel, a Watcher, was having the time of his life teaching humans how to make weapons to kill each other and how to strategize for war. Shemihaza taught humans sorcery and other things God hadn't meant for man to know, and this turned the world on its head.

The destruction from the Nephilim and their celestial fathers (the Watchers) was so bad that humans cried, and the archangels heard. Michael, Raphael, Uriel, and Gabriel looked down and saw the madness. They immediately sought God, letting Him know what was going on. They said to the Creator:

"Lord of lords, God of gods, King of kings, and God of the ages, the throne of Thy glory (standeth) unto all the generations of the ages, and Thy name holy and glorious and blessed unto all the ages! Thou hast made all things, and power over all things hast Thou: and all things are naked and open in Thy sight, and Thou seest all things, and nothing can hide from Thee."

They paid their respects to God before discussing what the angels were up to, demonstrating their loyalty to Him. First, they named Azazel, assigning him much blame for teaching the people of earth to be unrighteous, showing them eternal secrets of warfare and killing; that was even worse than the alchemy and sorcery that the angels had shared. He seemed far more invested in causing strife on earth than looking for beautiful women. It's clear to see that for once, it's not humanity sinning, but they're being instigated to do wrong things by the beings meant to steer them right.

The archangels defend humanity before God, making it clear that the chaos is all on the Watchers. They disclose information about the Nephilim as well. The archangels express their outrage at the violence and sin that's happening on earth, and their empathy for humanity is unmistakable. It's also interesting to note that they speak accusingly to God. After all, God knows all things before they happen, which means He knew this would happen and yet did nothing. This also shows us that while the archangels are close to God, they don't know the details of his plan and are about as helpless as we are when it comes to figuring out what comes next.

God tells Uriel to inform Noah that a flood will wipe out the world, and he needs to build an ark. If you're familiar with the story of Noah's ark from Genesis, you understand why God had to wipe out the world to get rid of the chaos the Watchers had wrought. God had found that Noah was the one righteous person of that period and wanted to keep him safe. The rest of humanity, it seemed, couldn't be trusted, as they had fallen for the Watchers' shenanigans.

God then commanded Raphael to seek out Azazel the Watcher and confront him for all the wrong he had done against humans. He was to bind the angel's feet and hands, cast him into darkness, then create an opening in the desert in Dudael, and cast him in there. Then Raphael was to put jagged rocks on the angel and cover him with darkness, then leave him in that place for all of eternity until the day of judgment when he would be thrown into the eternal fire.

God gave the archangels more instructions and proclaimed that the earth was healed, and that humanity wouldn't perish because of all the forbidden knowledge they had. It's not entirely clear whether God spoke specifically to Raphael or was issuing a command for the rest of the archangels, but he wanted the earth whole again. So, it's paradoxical that he asked the archangels to proclaim the earth's healing when he also wanted to flood it. It's theorized that he simply didn't want the corrupted humans to perish at the hands of the archangels. He wanted to take responsibility for what had happened by taking their lives with the flood but letting them into heaven since the sin wasn't really their fault.

Archangel Gabriel is then given the command to destroy the Nephilim, to cause them to turn on their own kind and destroy themselves in battle. Gabriel could turn the enemies of God against each other, and this was an easy thing to do since the Nephilim had already begun cannibalizing themselves. It's also interesting how Gabriel is less a messenger (as he is in the canonical Bible) and more a warrior like Michael. Equally fascinating is how his fighting style means his hands are technically free from bloodshed, as all he has to do is manipulate the Nephilim so that they war against each other.

God then turns his wrath on the big baddie, Shemihaza, and assigns Michael to capture him and all other remaining Watchers on earth. He tells Michael to bind them all, and after they have watched their own children kill each other, they are to be bound for 70 generations in valleys across the earth until their judgment day comes. It is speculated that God meant for them to be cast in the same place as Azazel. The fact that God wanted the Watchers to watch their sons rip themselves apart shows that the fallen angels might have held some paternal feelings for their children and would have been deeply hurt watching them murder each other that way.

Dee, Kelley and the Seven Secret Angels

The Enochian magic system that Dee and Kelley have given us was given to them by the angel Uriel. It has a magical square, in which there are seven secret angels: Gabriel, Michael, Raphael, Zadkiel, Zaphkiel, Haniel, and Camael. To be clear, the archangels are only seven in number, even though you might see their names differ from manuscript to manuscript.

Dee recorded hundreds of conversations with the angels from 1583 to 1587. One of the older records of these angelic communications began with a prayer where he clarified his motivation. He let on that ever since he was younger, he would pray for "pure sound wisdom and understanding of your (God's) truths, natural and artificial." He did all he could to acquire knowledge, to seek out the ultimate truth. He gathered every book, studied hard, and produced his theories, but he soon became exhausted with this method of seeking knowledge through optics, mathematics, history, geography, astrology, navigation, and all other areas he had mastered. They didn't give him the outcome he'd hoped for. He felt that the best way to get the answers he desired was to commune with angels, who would logically know them since they were only a step below God himself and would therefore be privy to the wisdom and knowledge of the Supreme Creator.

Dee was well aware that angels had communicated with Moses and Enoch in the past on God's behalf, letting them have the wisdom that he now desperately sought. Therefore, with this Biblical precedent set in his mind, he believed he could attain esoteric wisdom from these beings before the dawn of time. He wanted so badly to learn what Adam had once known and then lost upon his fall from grace. He knew that the angels would be able to provide the missing pieces to the arts of magic and divination, which were only very few pieces of the whole, pristine wisdom. So, to Dee, this thought process was very sound, both intellectually and spiritually. All he wanted was to bridge the divide between the error-filled human wisdom and the wisdom from God.

Dee had a room in his home that was consecrated for having conversations with the angels. He and Kelley would begin with a moment of silent prayer. Dee would ask God to send forth his angels, acknowledging God as the source of all wisdom and asking that he and Kelley be deemed worthy to receive understanding. Unlike other forms of medieval magic, they needed no incense, no hymns or incantations, rituals or ceremonies, candles, or charms to draw the planetary angels to them. All they had was a shew-stone, which the scryer would use to see the angels.

More Magic

It was Kelley who saw the angels and spoke to them, not Dee. All Dee did was ask questions and note down the responses the angels gave Kelley. With time, other ritual elements entered their conversations, whereas, in the beginning, it was just a scrying stone they needed. The angels spoke to the duo about a table of practice that they were to decorate with mystical symbols and wax discs on which they were to inscribe a seal of God. They were to place these discs beneath the table legs and under the shew stone on the table.

Many spirits came to Kelley, and they had many deep conversations. The more frequent visitors were Gabriel, Uriel, and Raphael. There was another regular besides those three named Madimi. They would appear as apparitions in different guises, sometimes as a red husbandman, a little girl, an old maid with yellow hair, or a tall, huge creature. As Kelley conversed with these celestial beings, two main kinds of knowledge were passed on to Dee. They gave him a lot of tables resembling grids that were supposed to be an angelic alphabet. These represented the language of divinity that would help Dee know the true nature of the universe. They also gave him the names of the angels and their roles, as well as the parts of the air they were in charge of, the angelic tribes they were from, and how many subordinates they ruled.

The information Dee received about angelic hierarchy was to give him charge over the angels and give him access to take part in the society of angels. Unfortunately, he was never able to move up the universal hierarchy with religious magic. The spiritual hierarchies and angelic language that he had been given weren't the actual pristine wisdom he wanted but simply a way to access the knowledge. Also, the hierarchy and language weren't fully complete, so he died without unlocking nature's secrets. Fortunately, he took meticulous notes on all he had done so that we could figure out for ourselves what he had been able to accomplish.

Chapter 6: Kabbalah 101

Kabbalah means "tradition," "reception," or "correspondence." It's an esoteric discipline, method, and school of thought in Jewish mysticism. A practitioner or Kabbalist is traditionally known as a *Mequbbal* in Judaism. The meaning of Kabbalah depends on the tradition and goals of the followers. It was originally a significant part of Judaism, but it's been adapted by Western esotericism with time. So, we now have the Hermetic Qabalah and the Christian Kabbalah.

The Hermetic Qabalah is the foundation of the philosophy of magical societies like the Thelemic orders and the Golden Dawn. It is also the foundation of mystical-religious societies like the Fellowship of the Rosy Cross and the Builders of the Adytum. During the Renaissance, it arose along with the Christian Kabbalah. The latter had also become popular because of the interest that Christian scholars had developed in the Jewish Kabbalah and its mystical principles, which they interpreted through the lens of Christian theology. The Christian scholars spelled the word as " Cabala " to distinguish it from both the Jewish and Hermetic Kabbalah.

Jewish Kabbalah consists of esoteric knowledge about the relationship between the constant, never-changing God and the ever-changing and mortal universe. God is Ein Sof, unknowable, mysterious, infinite, and immortal. His creation is the exact opposite of this.

Jewish Kabbalists had produced their own way to transmit sacred texts in the context of Jewish tradition and hark back to Jewish scriptures to lend more credence to their mystical, Kabbalistic teachings, which, for followers, are the definition of the intrinsic meaning of traditional rabbinic literature and the Hebrew Bible, as well as the aspects of them that were formerly unknown and kept secret. This is also the basis for all the religious observances of the Jews. The Zohar, one of the most significant kabbalistic texts, was published in the 13th century. Most practitioners stick with the Lurianic Kabbalah, which was named after Isaac Luria, a Jewish rabbi who came up with a new way to look at Kabbalistic philosophy that the faithful integrated with the Zohar's Kabbalah.

Traditional kabbalists believe that the Kabbalah's origins are from before the birth of religions in the world. They firmly believe that the Kabbalah is the foundation on which religions, philosophies, arts, sciences, and political systems were built. History has it that it came out of Jewish mysticism's earlier forms, originating sometime between the 12th and 13th centuries in Southern France and Spain. In the Ottoman Palestine of the 16th century, when the Jewish mystical renaissance was in force, the Kabbalah was reinterpreted. The patron of contemporary Kabbalah is Isaac Luria. From the 18th century until date, his Lurianic Kabbalah became very popular, particularly in Hasidic Judaism. By the 20th century, Gershom Scholem, a Jewish historian, led a wave of academic curiosity in the sacred Kabbalistic texts, which led to more research on the history of the Kabbalah in Judaic studies.

Kabbalistic Traditions

The Zohar has it that there are four ways to interpret the Torah. These four ways or levels are known as the pardes, based on the first letter of each one (PRDS). They are:

- *Peshat*, meaning direct and simple interpretations.
- *Remez*, being allegorical interpretations.
- *Derash*, referring to imaginative connections with similar verses and words.
- *Sod*, being the intrinsic, esoteric meanings.

Kabbalah followers understand that it is necessary to study the Torah along with the Kabbalah. For modern academic historians, the Kabbalah is about the specific doctrines that came out in the Middle Ages fully expressed in text. These historians stress the difference between that and the Merkabah mystical methods and ideas from before the texts. So, the early-modern Lurianic Kabbalah and the Zoharic Kabbalah of medieval times are both parts of Kabbalistic theory and make up the Kabbalah's Theosophical tradition. On the other hand, the Meditative-Ecstatic Kabbalah blends in the Medieval traditions.

There's a third tradition related to the Kabbalah – but it tends to be shunned – having to do with the magical goals of Practical Kabbalah. This is the part of Jewish mysticism that involves working with magic. It was okay only for the elite to work this white magic, as it was believed only they could handle it. Moshe Idel, a philosopher and historian of Romanian-Israeli descent, notes that the three models of the Kabbalah can be recognized working and competing for all through Jewish mysticism's history.

Theosophical Tradition of the Kabbalah

This tradition is also called the Theosophical-Theurgic tradition, with its focus solely on Luria and the Zohar. The goal is to grasp the realm of the divine and define it with the mythic and imaginative symbols of the experience of the human psyche. It relies more on intuition, compared to the Jewish philosophy, which is more rational. This is the central pillar of Kabbalah and is usually referred to when the word "kabbalah" is used. The theosophy points to the inner significant theurgic influence of our conduct as humans — the divine microcosm— on destroying or redeeming the spiritual world — the divine macrocosm. The point behind theosophical kabbalah is to lend metaphysical meaning to the religious practice in Judaism.

Ecstatic Kabbalah

This tradition is the meditative tradition of Ecstatic Kabbalah espoused by Isaac of Acre and Abraham Abulafia, which has the goal of uniting with God in a mystical sense. A good example of this form of Kabbalah is the Prophetic Kabbalah of Abulafia. Meditation here is founded on Maimonides' philosophy.

Magico-Talismanic Practical Kabbalah

The goal of this form of Kabbalah is to cause a change in both the physical and divine worlds through practical methods. While the theosophical view of worship was all about being in harmony with divine forces, Practical Kabbalah involves white magic, reserved only for the elite and those with pure intentions.

Traditional belief states that the prophets, patriarchs, and sages shared early kabbalistic knowledge orally, and with time these became a part of Jewish religious culture and literature. This view holds that around the 10th century BCE, early kabbalah was known to all and practiced by at least a million people across ancient Israel. When foreign powers conquered the land, the Jewish spiritual leaders (the Sanhedrin) hid what they knew of the kabbalah and kept it secret to avoid its misuse.

It's not easy to clarify or ascertain the precise ideas embodied by the Kabbalah. This is why you'll find different schools of thought on the matter, each with their own perspective. However, every perspective is accepted as valid. Halakhic authorities of modern times have done all they can to whittle down the diversity and scope within the practice of Kabbalah. They've tried to limit the study of the Kabbalah strictly to the Zohar and Lurianic teachings passed on from Isaac Luria to the faithful through Hayyim ben Joseph Vital.

All these attempts don't do much to clarify the depth and expression of this practice because those works also have commentaries on Albotonian writings, *Abulafian* writings, the *Sefer Yetzirah,* and the *Berit Menuhah,* which marries theosophical and ecstatic mysticism. So, you need to keep in mind that matters like the *sephirot* (the Kabbalah's 10 emanations or attributes through which Ein Sof is revealed and through which the physical and metaphysical realms are continually created) should be considered very abstract and interpreted intuitively.

Jewish and Non-Jewish Kabbalah

During and after the Renaissance, the Kabbalah texts became popular in non-Jewish culture. Hermetic occultists and Christian Hebraists studied and translated them, which led to the Hermetic Qabalah and the Christian Cabala. Both groups used the Jewish ideas generously and merged them with other religious traditions, theologies, and magical associations. As Christian Cabala died out in the Age of Reason, Hermetic Qabalah flourished underground in Western esotericism. As a result of non-Jewish ties with divination, alchemy, and magic, Kabbalah soon took on some occult ideas that were not allowed in Judaism, which held that Practical Kabbalah wasn't central to religion and was only restricted to some of the elite. Today, many literary works on the Kabbalah are from the occult and New Age traditions of Cabala and don't give a clear depiction of the original Judaic Kabbalah. Instead, you'll find traditional and academic Jewish works that translate and expand upon the Judaic Kabbalah to boost readership.

History and Origins of Jewish Mysticism

Kabbalah, as it is traditionally understood, originated in Eden. It was revealed to elect tzadikim (meaning "righteous people') from a distant past and was largely preserved by a select few. According to contemporary scholarship, it would appear that different schools of Jewish mysticism came up at various periods in the history of the Jews. All of them showed older forms and the cultural and intellectual environment of that period in history. Note that it's not easy to answer questions regarding influence, lineage, transmission, and innovation, and any answers gleaned would not be consistent.

It was originally believed that Kabbalistic knowledge was the bedrock of the Oral Torah given to Moses around the 13th century BCE by God on Mount Sinai. Others believe that the Kabbalah is much older than that, having begun with Adam.

For some centuries, the esoteric knowledge of the Kabbalah was known by its practice — meditation *Hitbonenut, Hitbodedut,* meaning "isolating yourself" or "being alone," or *Nevu'a,* which is a word to describe the goal of this isolation: Prophecy. According to Aryeh Kaplan (a Kabbalistic scholar), you can trace the roots of the Kabbalistic meditative practices of medieval times to the oral transmissions of the Biblical Prophetic tradition.

When the Tanakh words were edited and subsequently canonized from the 5th century BCE, and the occult knowledge had been encoded in various scrolls and writings, esoteric knowledge was called *Ma'aseh* Merkavah — meaning "the act of the Chariot" — and *Ma'aseh B'reshit* — meaning "the act of Creation." Merkabah mysticism made references to encoded knowledge and meditation methods in the book of Ezekiel the prophet, where he describes the vision he had of the "Divine Chariot." B'reshit mysticism made references to Genesis Chapter 1 in the Torah, which is said to have the secrets of the universe (which John Dee desperately sought) as well as the forces of nature.

In Second Temple Judaism, upon returning from Babylon, certainty about Prophetic revelation shifted to the exegesis and canonization of the holy writings after Ezra the Scribe. What remained was Ruach HaKodesh, the lower prophecy level, with esoteric divine secrets, angelic revelations, and eschatological deliverance from Roman and Greek influences that oppressed Apocalyptic literature like the Qumranic Dead Sea Scrolls and the Book of Daniel.

Mysticism in the Torah

The Torah discusses the creation story from the book of Genesis, and it shows mysteries of Ein Sof, the garden of Eden, Adam's and Eve's true nature, the Tree of Life, and the Tree of the Knowledge of Good and Evil. It also covers the interactions between the Serpent and other supernatural beings, which then led to the great sin of eating the forbidden fruit.

The prophet Ezekiel's visions had inspired a lot of mystical speculation, just as Isaiah's vision in the Temple and the vision Jacob had of the ladder that led to heaven. Moses' experiences with God on Mount Sinai and with the burning bush also serve as evidence of the mystical occurrences in the Torah that are the root of Jewish mysticism.

God's 72-letter name, used in meditation, comes from the Hebrew words Moses spoke to an angel as the Sea of Reeds parted so that the Hebrews could get away from their enemies. The Exodus miracle that led to Moses being given the Ten Commandments and the Jewish Orthodox perspective of the reception of the Torah on Mount Sinai came before the first Jewish nation was created – around 300 years before King Saul.

Kabbalah in Medieval Europe

Scholars have found that there were several Kabbalistic brotherhoods in Europe as far back as the 12th century. Some, like the Unique Cherub Circle and the Iyyun Circle, were esoteric and remained anonymous. Theosophical Kabbalistic ideas were first documented in the latter part of the 1100s in Southern France, among the Sages of Provence and Languedoc. This happened concurrently with the appearance of the *Bahir* or "Book of Brightness" that describes Ein Sof's sephirot traits.

Kabbalah then moved on to north-east Spain in Catalonia, around 1194 to 1270, focusing on the upper sephirot. Following that, the doctrine fully expressed itself in the latter part of the 1200s among Kabbalists of Castilia, especially with the Book of Splendor (the Zohar). At this time, it was mostly about healing the dualities of Gnosticism between God's lower revealed female and male attributes.

Most Orthodox Jews refuse to accept that the Kabbalah has been developed over the years. Exoteric Judaism's Elder Sages (called the Rishonim) were a small part of Kabbalistic practices, and it is they who gave the Jewish mystical practice scholarly acceptance. Once the Zohar had been made available to the masses in the 13th century, the word "Kabbalah" morphed to represent the teachings that came from the Zohar's teachings and then morphed again to represent the teachings of the Zohar as expounded by Isaac Luria.

The Hekhalot and Merkabah

The mystical teachings and methods of texts known as the Hekhalot (meaning "heavenly chambers') and Merkabah (meaning "divine chariot') remained from the 1st century BCE to the 10th century CE and then eventually gave way to the Kabbalah in its documented manuscript form. The heroes of the text are Rabbinic Judaism's Talmudic Sages. From the 8th to the 11th century, the *Sefir Yetzirah* and the *Hekhalot* texts found their way to European Jews.

John Dee and Kabbalah

Dee was committed to the Kabbalah. He spent a few years in Prague when Rabbi Judah Loew's golem rites were at their height. On June 27, 1589, Dr. Henricus Khunrath of Hamburg visited Dee while he was at Bremen, Germany. The latter had significantly influenced the former's occult work, *The Amphitheatre of Eternal Wisdom,* an engraving with occult symbols carved into it. The engravings were representations of Dee's outlook as he discussed it in *Monas hieroglyphica,* a combination of alchemical, Cabalist, and mathematical ideas that the adept can use to gain insight into nature.

In Western history, Dee was the first scientist to be concretely connected to a Satanic praxis rooted in the Kabbalah. Dee received Kabbalistic philosophy from Rabbi Judah Loew and then passed that knowledge on to some of the most forward-thinking scientists, theologians, and mathematicians of the time. This was done through the Rosicrucians, which was founded on a combination of Protestantism and Kabbalistic teachings.

Some of the most powerful rulers and aristocrats protected and patronized this fraternity, including Frederick V, King of Bohemia, who headed the Protestant Union. This form of Protestantism had been in the making for years and was nurtured by secret powers across Europe. It was a movement that was meant to resolve the religious issues they faced at the time using mysticism, particularly with Cabalistic and Hermetic influences.

The Rosicrucians wanted to convince the most devout Protestants that the divinity of Judaism was very real, evident in the philosophy of the Kabbalah. They also wanted to convince the intellectuals and scientists of the potential of the Kabbalah to lead man to his inner godhood. Using the words "scientists" and "Protestants" this way isn't meant to show that there's some division between the two, as in atheists versus religionists. This was Europe in the 17th century, which means that most scientists were also Christians. The Kabbal continued to find its way around Europe and devoted worship of God, blended with science and magic.

By the 18th century, some of the intelligentsia had come to accept the Kabbalah. The 1614 Rosicrucian manifesto *(The Fama)* connects the Kabbalah with people "Imbued with great wisdom," who had made it their sole purpose to innovate and streamline all arts till they were perfect enough for humans to know how noble they are. The Monas *hieroglyphica,* written by John Dee, also heavily influenced the "Brief Consideration" published along with *The Confessio* (1615). The secret philosophy upon which the manifestos of the Rosicrucians were written is based on John Dee's philosophy. The secret philosophy was the rabbinic teachings that had been given in the Kabbalistic texts. It was the "repair of the world," or the *tikkun olam,* where the Judaized man could take on the powers of God to "correct" a "flawed and imperfect" creation.

Chapter 7: Enochian Ceremonial Magick

Enochian magick is ceremonial magick. The "k" is added to the word "magic" to clarify that it's the ceremonial sort of magic. John Dee's Watchtower tablets were heavily influenced by the tradition of the Jewish Merkavah, which was a mystical system that taught people about God's Chariot or Throne. God's Throne — *the Merkavah* — is described in the Book of Ezekiel (particularly Chapter 1) and the book of the Revelation of Saint John (chapter 4). The mystics of Renaissance Christianity, like John Dee, were very interested in Merkavah tradition, so the books mentioned above definitely influenced him to some degree.

Breaking Down the WatchTower Tablets

The Watchtower tablets are a metaphor for the Four Great Kherubim of the Elements. Dee writes in his diaries when the angels first describe the Watchtowers to him before he was given their letters or structure:

Ave: "The Four houses are the Four Angels of the Earth, which are the Four Overseers, and Watchtowers, that... God... hath placed against the... Great Enemy, the Devil."

The above sentence is key to understanding what the Watchtowers are all about and the angelic beings connected to them. You must first remember that the Grimoiric perspective did nothing to separate the Zodiac from the Earthly Elements, as is the convention today. Instead, it set the Zodiac Triplicities in charge of the Elements and proclaimed that these Elements originated from them as well. According to Agrippa, Fire was linked to the East, not just in the sky but also in the Four Winds. In Ezekiel, it is written:

"And the likeness of the firmament upon the heads of the living creatures was as the likeness of an expanse of awesome ice, stretched forth over their heads above. And under the firmament were their wings straight, the one toward the other: every one had two, which covered on this side, and every one had two, which covered on that side, their bodies."

The Kherubim — The Chaioth ha Qadesh — are the ones who support the sky. They are Pillars, holding the world as we know it above the Abyss waters. These pillars are found across all cultures and have been there for most of history. This is what the Watchtowers are. The four Sigils are the signatures of these Kherubim themselves, and the tablets hold drawings that capture the essences of the Beasts spoken of in Revelation: *"And the four beasts had each of them six wings about him, and they were full of stars within."* It also says, *"And round about the Throne were four and twenty seats; and upon the seats, I saw four and twenty Elders sitting, clothed in white raiment; and They had on Their heads crowns of gold."*

These 24 Elders are connected to the 12 Zodiacs, with two per Zodiac sign. As each Triplicity has three signs, that means each Element has six Elders. So, for Fire, there are two Elders of Sagittarius, two of Leo, and Two of Aries. So, the "six wings full of stars" that each Kherub has referred to are the Zodiacal Powers that the Elders embody, the latter being governed by the Kherub. This is visible on the Watchtowers, where you have six Elder Names written across each one. The tablet represents the Kherub, and the Elders are the six wings of that Kherub.

Three Divine Names rule each tablet. Each of these names is connected to a Zodiac sign, according to Enochian scholars. This information, sadly, wasn't told to Dee, so we can only speculate as to its validity. Altogether, the three could be considered as Elemental, meaning they are the Divine Names used to summon

Fire. However, they are chiefly about the stars. The direction matters with the Watchtowers, just as you would expect it to with other grimoiric magick systems. It takes precedence over the element(s) that may be linked with the direction in question.

However, there's a Divine Name that could be purely Elemental. The East Triplicity has Fire as its Spirit or Essence. As Ezekiel writes:

"Now, as I beheld the living creatures, behold one wheel upon the earth by the living creatures, with his four faces. [...] Whithersoever the spirit was to go, they went, thither was their spirit to go; and the wheels were lifted up over against them: for the spirit of the living creature was in the wheels. When those went, these went; and when those stood, these stood; and when those were lifted up from the earth, the wheels were lifted up over against them: for the spirit of the living creatures was in the wheels."

The Essence of the Kherub is within the wheel, and each Watchtower has a Divine Name that rests in its heart in a round pattern, much like a spiral. This is known as the Watchtower's King, and it's the tablet's Elemental Force. The Wheels are known as *Auphanim* and are an Angelic Order. They were known in Medieval times as "Galgalim," meaning "spirals" or "swirlings." These are the traditional Zodiac angels. Ezekiel writes, *"As for their rims, they were so high that they were dreadful; and their rims were full of stars round about them four."*

This is the four-fold Zodiac Wheel. The Wheel of Fire which holds the Kherub's Essence rules the Zodiac's Fire Triplicity. The Divine Names are used to rule and summon the Zodiacal Elders, who are Auphanic Rulers. Ezekiel also writes, *"The appearance of the wheels and their work was like unto the color of a beryl: and they four had one likeness: and their appearance and their work were as it were a wheel in the midst of a wheel."*

This is most likely a night sky description. Beryl's color resembles the deep blue of outer space. If one follows the horizon line, the sky looks like a massive wheel lying on its side. You'll notice that in horoscope charts, this is how the sky is often depicted. Despite this, the zodiac belt arcs across the sky from one skyline to the next, as if it were a massive vertical wheel contained within the sky's horizontal wheel. It's a wheel inside a wheel.

We observe the "King" Name (a wheel) in the middle of the Elders' Names (also a wheel) in Dee's Watchtowers. The center of the Wheel is the "King" Name, and its six spokes are the Elders. This also shows that the Elders of Revelation and Ezekiel's Wheels are both identical, at least in Enochian Magick.

The Watchtowers are the manifestation of the four Chaioth Ha Qadesh and their Wheels, as stated by Ezekiel and St. John, both of them Merkavah Mystics. All of the aforementioned is primarily concerned with the Zodiac and exists on the outskirts of the Chockmah, which is the Magickal Universe. This would encompass the complete Great Cross of each Tablet, which comprises the Kherubs' own wings and wheels.

In light of the foregoing, it could be that each Watchtower's four "sub-quadrants" are the portions of the Kherubs that touch our Earth in Malkuth. The four sub-quadrants correspond to Ezekiel's four Faces of the Kherubs, as he writes:

"Also out of the midst thereof came the likeness of four living creatures. And this was their appearance; they had the likeness of a man. And every one had four faces, and every one had four wings [...], And they had the hands of a man under their wings on their four sides, and the four had their faces and their wings. Their wings were joined one to another; they turned not when they went; they went every one straightforward. As for the likeness of their faces, they four had the face of a man, and the face of a lion to the right: and they four had the face of an ox on the left side; they four also had the face of an eagle."

In the Watchtowers, where the six Elder Names are gathered together atop the four arms of a cross, Ezekiel writes of four wings (as opposed to six in John's Vision.

It could be that the "Parts of the Earth" (as depicted on the Watchtower Tablets) symbolize the Firmament supported by the Kherubs, and on which rests the Throne. Also, John mentions the Powers of the Seven Spirits (Archangels) of God in Revelation, and they could be represented by the Heptarchia component of Dee's scheme. So, this is the whole Merkavah Vision and the Enochian system's very foundation.

Dee was informed by the angel AVE, through Kelley, about the purpose of the Watchtowers. Here is Ave's response, as exactly noted by Dee:

Ave: Now to the purpose. Rest, for the place is Holy. First, generally what this Tablet Containeth.

> 1) All human knowledge.
>
> 2) Out of it, springeth Physick.
>
> 3) The knowledge of the Elemental Creatures among you. How many kids there are, and for what use they were created. Those that live in the air by themselves. Those that live in the waters by themselves. Those that live on the earth by themselves. The property of fire—which is the secret life of all things.
>
> 4) The knowledge, finding, and use of Metals. The virtues of them. The congelations and virtues of Stones. They [these preceding three things] are all of one matter.
>
> 5) The conjoining and knitting together of Natures. The destruction of Nature and of things that may perish.
>
> 6) Moving from place to place (as into this Country, of that Country at pleasure.]
>
> 7) The knowledge of all crafts Mechanical.
>
> 8) Transmutatio formalis, sed non-essentialis [formal alchemical transmutation.]
>
> 9) [Dee's note in margin:] The ninth chapter may be added and is of the secrets of men knowing, whereof there is a particular table.

Chapter 8: The Heptarchia Mystica — Angelic Sigils and Magical Tools

In Dee's later years, he had decided to hide his work in a large cedar chest, in a hidden compartment. The chest was bought from his estate and had several owners, and the documents were only discovered in 1662 and then passed on to Elias Ashmole ten years later. Eventually, it moved on to the British Library.

Ashmole reported that half of the records in that hidden compartment were accidentally ruined by a maid before they found them and tried to preserve what was rest. Still, the records of Dee's work from 1581 to 1585 remain mostly intact. The records are so detailed that it takes a fair bit of time and diligence to separate the useful from what's not needed.

A lot of the communication was vital in terms of magical operations but had no direct relevance or significance when it came to the magic systems. There are periods in which Dee and Kelley didn't get much valuable information. It seemed the magicians had simply continued to interact with the angels to keep up the routine. The angels gave the men some celestial gossip, prophecies, and visions, but nothing solid. Also, they would go off on a tangent discussing Elizabethan politics and apocalyptic religion, the personal problems Kelley and Dee had, and irrelevant questions Dee had adamantly included in the work.

So, their work can be split chronologically into three periods that had the meat of the magic system we know as Enochian magick, which were separated by months of not-so-valuable information. The third period is the one that is strictly "Enochian," but it's a term also used to describe the rest of the work.

The First Period: The Heptarchia Mystica

This was the first magic system that Dee received from the angels. It's a fairly complex and self-contained form of planetary angel magic. In terms of style, it resembles several Solomonic grimoires, but that's where the similarity ends. The content is vastly different. You can find the entire record of the Heptarchia's presentation in Dee's *Mysteriorum Libri Quinti. De Haptarchia Mystica* is a working grimoire made up of Dee's observations from that record. Some of the angelic conversations can be found in Casaubon's *A True and Faithful Relationship*. The British Museum is in possession of these manuscripts.

The magic was presented in an orderly and sequential manner in comparison to the work that came later. It talked about the vital physical tools needed for this magic and then followed that up with the hierarchy of the 49 "Good Angels," as well as information about the Ministers, Princes, and Kings of this hierarchy. The main part of this information came through to Dee during 1582, and in the following year's spring, they had made vital corrections to the equipment's design after a brief hiatus in the magical work and the Liber Loagaeth's presentation.

Magical Tools

While it's not clear whether Kelley or Dee worked the magic they were given, we know that the angels instructed them to create certain magical items, which for some reason, were nearly completely ignored by Crowley and the Golden Dawn. These items are vital for the practicing Enochian Magician. They are:

- The Ring
- The Holy Table
- The Ensigns of Creation

The Sigillum Dei Aemeth

Through all John Dee's artifacts and writings, the *Sigillum Dei Aemeth*, also called the Seal of the Truth of God, is the most popular. The sigil shows up in works much older than Dee's, and it appears he was familiar with them, but he was dissatisfied with them. So, he reached out to the angels to give him guidance as he created his version.

Dee had inscribed the sigil on circular tablets made of wax. He had set four other tablets beneath the table's legs and one on the table. As he communed with the angels through Kelley and the shew stone, he received instruction on how to create them. Subsequently, he would use the tablets as part of his preparations for the rituals to allow further clearer communication with the angels.

In popular culture, there have been various renditions of the Sigillum Dei Aemeth used in television shows like Supernatural to trap demons, making it so that they would be unable to leave once the sigil contained them. That's only on television, though.

Enochian magic is an angelic magic system that is grounded in the number 7. This number is also linked very strongly to the seven traditional planets. For this reason, the Sigillum Dei Aemeth is mainly made up of stars with seven points (heptagrams) and seven-sided polygons (heptagons).

The Outer Ring: This is made up of the names of seven angels, with each one linked to a planet. To find the name of an angel, you begin with a capital letter on the ring. If that letter has a number above it, then count that same number of letters clockwise. If there's a number beneath the letter, count that number of letters counterclockwise. Continue this way, and you will find the following names:

- Aaoth (Mercury)
- Innon (Venus)
- Thaaoth (Mars)

- Geethog (Jupiter)
- Galaas (Saturn)
- Galethog (Moon)
- Horlwn (Sun)

Together, these are known as the Angels of Brightness. They are the ones who "grasp the seven inward powers of God," who no one but God himself knows.

Galethog: Within the outer ring, you'll find seven symbols that create the word Galethog, with the letters "th" represented by just one sigil. You can read the name in reverse. These are the seven sigils that are called "the Seats of the One and everlasting GOD." These 7 secret Angels come from every cross and letter formed. In substance, they represent the father. In their form, they represent the son. Within, they reflect the Holy Spirit.

The Outer Heptagon: These names of the seven angels who always remain in the presence of God is connected with a planet, and written in a 7 by 7 grid, vertically. When you read the grid horizontally, you'll unlock the seven names of the outer heptagon. Here are the original names:

- Michael (Mercury)
- Haniel (Venus)
- Cumael (Mars)
- Zadkiel (Jupiter)
- Zaphkiel (Saturn)
- Gabriel (Moon)
- Raphael (Sun)

These new names are to be written clockwise.

The Central Structures: The five levels that follow are rooted in another grid of letters, also 7 by 7. You can read each in various directions. The letters form names of more spirits of planets, which were first written in a zigzag manner, beginning from the upper left corner. In each name, the "el" portion was taken out to create the grid. The names are:

- Corabiel (Mercury)
- Nogahel (Venus)
- Madimiel (Mars)
- Zedekieiel (Jupiter)
- Sabathiel (Saturn)
- Lebanael (Moon)
- Semeliel (Sun)

The names between the heptagram and the outer heptagon are seen when you read the grid horizontally. These are the names of God that are unknown to the angels and which man can neither read nor speak.

The names you find in the heptagram's points are the Daughters of Light. The Sons of Light are the names within the heptagram's lines. The names that sit between both central heptagons are known as the Daughters of the Daughters and the Sons of the Sons.

The Pentagram: Around the pentagram, the angelic, planetary spirits repeat. The letters that spell out "Sabathiel" have the "el" removed, and the rest on the outside are scattered. The five spirits are spelled out, but they're closer to the middle. Each name's first letter lies within one of the pentagram's points. In the very middle is Levanael, around a cross that represents the earth.

The Ring

The angels made it clear that the magician could do nothing without the Ring. According to a passage from Dee's notes on Wednesday, March 14, 1582, the archangel Michael stretched out his sword with his right arm and asked Kelley to look. Then the sword split in two, and out of it came a great fire from which Michael took out a ring.

He handed the ring over to Uriel as he said:

"The strength of God is unspeakable. Praised be God forever and ever... After this sort must thy ring be: Note it." Archangel Michael also added, "I will reveal thee this ring: which was never revealed since the death of Salomon: with whom I was present. I was present with him in strength and mercy. Lo, this is it. This is it, wherewith all Miracles, and divine works and wonders were wrought

by Salomon: This is it, which I have revealed unto thee. This is it, which Philosophie dreameth of. This is it, which the Angels scarce know. This is it, and blessed be his Name: yea, his Name be blessed forever... So shall it do, at thy commandment. Without this, thou shalt do nothing. Blessed be his name, that cumpasseth all things: Wonders are in him, and his Name is WONDERFULL: His Name worketh wonders from generation, to generation."

The Ring was made of gold, engraved with a seal, and had a circle in the middle of the seal. On top of the circle was a V, and on the bottom was an L. Through the circle was a horizontal line that extended outside the circle's circumference. This was all on a square with four letters: P, E, L, and E, starting from the top left corner and moving clockwise around each corner of the square. The word "Pele" is Latin for "He will work wonders."

It was a huge deal to have been given a ring once used by the archetypal magician himself, King Solomon. This ring is the same one he used to control even demons. While the ring's design was unique, the word Pele was in Dee's two books in his possession, *Occult Philosophy* by Cornelius Agrippa and *De Verbo Mirifico* by Johann Reuchlin. The authors were, respectively, a Hebrew scholar and German humanist. Agrippa got the word from Reuchlin, it appears.

The ring is to be of pure gold. While not all of us know how to create a ring of gold, let alone have the funds to have one made, you can make one out of a poster board or colored paper. It's nowhere near being golden, and you may think it's silly or would have no effect, but the fact is that it isn't the material itself that makes the magic, but the magician. Doubting and questioning will give you no results. To work with the paper ring, you can repeat what Michael said about the ring to Dee as a prayer and then put it on.

The Lamen

The Lamen is inextricably connected to the Holy Table. When you wear the Lamen over your heart, it connects you to the Holy Table. You must know what both items represent; otherwise, putting on the Lamen and taking a seat at the Holy Table is a pointless gesture.

The designs of these items were derived from the letters of the names of the Heptarchy angels. While it's not clear which one they got first, it makes sense to start off discussing the Lamen. The traditional Lamen is a breastplate. You hang it from your neck with a ribbon or a chain. Its archetype is the breastplate worn by Israel's High Priest. It's a square plate with a 3 by 4 grid, in which are embedded 12 precious gems, each one representing the 12 tribes of Israel and the 12 signs of the Zodiac. The Lamen given to Kelley and Dee had no precious stones, but they had 84 letters of the angelic alphabet arranged precisely and interestingly.

Dee and Kelley had received two versions. The first one came to them in 1582 and was a weird combination of squiggles, lines, and letters that resembled Goetic or Solomonic sigils. They were told that it had to be made of gold and was meant to be protected. When they got it, for the remainder of the year and even part of 1583, they got material from the angels regarding the 49 Good Angels. The angel names had seven letters and were derived by a complex process of arranging letters from a table shaped like a cross made up of 7 by 7 tables, forming 343 squares in total, with each square possessing a letter and a number. The magicians were taught to arrange these letters to form the hierarchy of planetary angels. Each planetary sphere (7 in number) is assigned five ministers, a prince, and a king. The 343 letters create the names of the 49 good angels and are sorted according to planets, beginning from the top of the wheel and moving counterclockwise. The only names in capital letters are the kings and princes.

Below are the names of the 49 good angels, with their seven princes and 35 ministers:

Venus:

   1) King BALIGON
   2) Prince BORNOGO
   3) Minister Bapnido
   4) Minister Besgeme
   5) Minister Blumapo
   6) Minister Bmamgal
   7) Minister Basldedf

Sol (The Sun)

   8) King BOBOGEL
   9) Prince BEFAFES

10) Minister Basmelo
11) Minister Bernole
12) Minister Branglo
13) Minister Brisfli
14) Minister Bnagole

Mars

15) King BABALEL
16) Prince BVTMONO
17) Minister Bazpama
18) Minister Blintom
19) Minister Bragiop
20) Minister Bermale
21) Minister Bonefon

Jupiter

22) King BYNEPOR
23) Prince BLISDON
24) Minister Balceor
25) Minister Belmara
26) Minister Benpagi
27) Minister Barnafa
28) Minister Bmilges

Mercury

29) King BNASPOL
30) Prince BRORGES
31) Minister Baspalo
32) Minister Binodab
33) Minister Bariges
34) Minister Binofon
35) Minister Baldago

Saturn

36) King BNAPSEN
37) Prince BRALGES
38) Minister Bormila
39) Minister Buscnab
40) Minister Bminpol
41) Minister Bartiro
42) Minister Bliigan

Luna (the Moon)

43) King BLVMAZA
44) Prince BAGENOL
45) Minister Bablibo
46) Minister Busduna
47) Minister Blingef
48) Minister Barfort
49) Minister Bamnode

Sadly, the part of Dee's material that was meant to explain how to summon these kings, ministers, and princes did not survive. We do know that after they had gotten the sigils, names, and hierarchical structures of the 49 angels, Dee and Kelley were told that the Lamen they first received was fake, given to them by a meddling spirit. They were then given instructions on making a new one that wasn't meant for protection this time around but to make the magicians worthy of performing this magic.

Creating the Lamen and Holy Table

The main key to creating the Lamen is a 12 by 7 table with the letters of the heptarchic princes and kings of the seven planets. Imitating the Big Bang's cooling phase, the 12 by 7 table is a condensed form of the 343 squares from the bigger, cross-like table. The right half of the table has the kings' names, while the left half has the princes' names. For each planet, the kings' and princes' names are not on the same line. For instance, King Bobogel of the sun is aligned with prince Bornogo of Venus, rather than being on the same line as prince Befafes. This seeming lack of symmetry is balanced out to form the Holy Table.

The Lamen is a table with 24 squares, sorted from top to bottom. You have 2 squares, stacked above 4, then 6, then another row of 6 atop a row of 4 that rests above a final row of 2 squares. This is then enclosed in a diamond square that is within a square, subsequently enclosed by a larger square.

To get the letters of the table that were applied to the Lamen, you'd have to divide the table into three parts, named flesh, heart, and skin. Then the letters are moved to the blank Lamen in three steps:

1) The flesh letters are added to the Lamen's perimeter as they appear on the 12 by 7 table.

2) The heart letters are added to the next inner square's corner inconsistently and oddly.

3) The corners of the skin letters are added to the innermost diamond square's corners in a way that matches their spots on the 12 by 7 table. Next, the remaining letters of the 12 by 7 table (24 in number) are interwoven into the rest of the squares in the middle of the Lamen.

Then, Dee was told to translate the letters of the completed Lamen from Latin to Angelic script. Just like with the Ring, it was suggested that gold be used for the Lamen. Also, like the Ring, you can just use a poster board or paper and laminate it with plastic to keep it safe. To hang it around your neck, puncture a small hole or two at the top and thread a ribbon through it. As you hang it around your neck, pray:

> Here is the Lamen. As the Holy Table connects Heaven and Earth,
>
> may this Lamen that I now place over my beating heart connect me to the Holy Table.

The Holy Table

Renaissance magicians had always been familiar with magick tables. The purpose of the magick table is to make the entire space you're using for your ritual's holy ground, which is way better than using the protective circle or triangle that only consecrates the area within the shape. The table is the Holy of Holies, where divinity and humanity meet.

Before Dee met Kelley, he already had a table for his magical practices, but after the development of his magic, it was clear that the angels wanted Dee to change his table. They wanted the table to be constructed from "Sweetwood," exactly two cubits high and two cubits square. It was to be an "instrument of conciliation." The table was to be set on a red silk carpet that would also have the scryer's chair on it. After setting the Seven Ensigns of Creation and the Sigillum Dei Aemeth, red silk would be used to cover the Holy Table. The difference between the silk on the floor and the one covering the Holy Table is that the latter has tassels of gold hanging from its corners. Then the black mirror or scrying stone was to be set on the Sigillum.

The Wand

The wand is a vital magical instrument. It uses your Magical Will and channels the wisdom of the divine through you. It focuses on your magical faculties to get the results you desire from your spells and rituals. You use the wand for evocations and invocations. This simple El wand used in Enochian magic houses your creative force as well. When you charge it with masculine energy, it represents the mystical lingam. In the Enochian magic system, the wand represents the element of Fire and is often used for the magical operations involving the Fire Watchtower. Some magicians use the wand, while others prefer to use just the crystal ball as Kelley did.

The Seven Ensigns of Creation

In a footnote to *Quinti Libri Mysteriorum: Liber Tertius*, Dee writes, *"Of these seven tables, characters, or scutcheons. Consider the words spoken in the fifth book Anno 1583, April 2nd. How they are proper to every King and prince in their order. They are Instruments of Conciliation."*

The Seven Ensigns of Creation are essentially planetary talismans that are to be on the Holy Table, set up in a circle around the Sigillum Dei Aemeth or in a straight line along the table's edge closest to the scryer. They were inspired by the Goetia and the *Lemegeton.* They were made of purified tin or simply painted onto the table. Like the Holy Table and the Lamen, they are "Instruments of Conciliation" linked to the planetary princes and kings.

Five of the ensigns are square tables with squares filled with lines, crosses, letters, and numbers. Two are a circle with a square around it. The letter B — written as Pa in the angelic alphabet — is the letter most used in the ensigns. Originally, they were Latin letters, but the angel later insisted that they be replaced with angelic characters. Dee wasn't eager to do this at first and had asked the angel if it was absolutely necessary, but the angel insisted. It's not clear whether or not Dee complied.

The ensigns are to be used in rituals. The magician can hold them in their hand when invoking entities or praying. However, there is no clarity on how exactly this works, as no records exist to explain the process. Still, they should remain part of your practice as they are a vital part of the hierarchical current that flows into the Enochian temple's holy ground. You can recreate the ensigns using the paper board or any other material available to you. Set the ensigns close to points of the Sigillum. There is a lot of information on the magical tools of Enochian magic, so much that it couldn't possibly be contained in this book. So, you are encouraged to do some more studying if you're serious about practicing this magic.

Chapter 9: Liber Loagaeth

The second vital phase of Dee and Kelley's work is quite the mystery and spanned 1582 to 1583. There was a fair bit of tension between both magicians, which, oddly, allowed for the incredible body of work called *Liber Mysteriorum Sextus et Sanctus, the Book of Enoch*, and *Liber Loagaeth* at various times in history. While Enochian scholars try their best to help us examine all the data from this work, it's not enough to help modern Enochian magicians create a system they can work with from this material.

One reason that not enough attention is given to this phase of Dee's work is the nature of the book itself and its lack of clear direction on how it should be practiced. Also, the work from this period is very focused on Dee's obsession with finding the Bible's lost books, the Apocrypha, and the *Book of Enoch* in particular, which shows up in several parts of the canonical Bible. The result is that the *Liber Loagaeth* is full of rhetoric that sounds prophetic and has lots of apocalyptic images. In recent times, some commentators have looked upon the book as being sectarian. They even claim that the material has sinister goals. They believe that it is Lovecraftian or Satanic and that the angels aren't quite what they claim to be.

Everyone is allowed their own opinion when it comes to matters of spirituality. All aspects of spirituality can be likened to a pallet full of different paint colors, and it's up to the artist — the magician — to figure out what to make of it. They could paint a wondrous, beautiful landscape or something out of hell. It's really up to you.

However, it would be wise to recall that the material Dee and Kelley have given us was based on questions that Englishmen asked from the 16th century who had framed them in the context of the Bible. So, we're listening in on these conversations and gaining answers that were given in the only form that they could understand the message at the time – framed against a Biblical backdrop. In other words, if Dee happened to be an African from Yoruba land, he would likely have used language that pertained to the Orisha tradition, and the angels would have passed along their message in the same way so he could grasp the essence.

An Immense Body of Work

The Liber Loagaeth has 48 leaves, each with lettered squares of 49 x 49, with 115,000 lettered squares in total. Each square is filled with letters in line with Kelley's vision, creating the 49 calls in the angelic tongue. These leaves were dictated to the magicians by Galvah, Nalvage, and other angels. Note, the angelic letters aren't the same as the ones in angelic language that came later and became the cornerstone of the Enochian phase of Dee and Kelley's work.

Loagaeth means "speech from God." Both magicians were told that the 49 calls were the very words God uttered at the beginning of creation. They claimed it's the same language Adam spoke when he named all living creatures. Sadly, the calls were either never translated, or the material with their translations has been destroyed or lost. Modern linguists have done their best, but they still can't find any guideposts that could lead to a well-formed language to class the Loagaeth calls on the same level as the angelic language of the final phase of these magicians' partnership.

Kelly went all in with his visionary skills, and what he saw was often characterized by dazzling light that was so bright even Dee could see it as well. The light would leap out of the scrying stone to penetrate Kelley's head and send him into a trance. From this altered state of consciousness, Kelly could read *Liber Loagaeth's* text and understand it fully as well. However, the angels absolutely forbade him from translating it and were informed that God would give the translations himself later. By the end of their sessions, the light that leaped onto Kelly's head would leave and head back to the stone. Then Kelley would come back to regular consciousness, and he had no memory of what had happened each time.

The Alphabet of Angels

Giving a clear chronology of what transpired with Dee and Kelley's visionary events is difficult because of the corrections and amendments that were made to some parts of the magical systems, and the same is the case with the angelic alphabet.

Both magicians received the angelic alphabet during the Loagaeth phase of their work. Since they were asked to replace the English or Latin letters of the Holy Table, Lamen, and Seven Ensigns of Creation with the angelic letters, this influence inevitably affected the Heptarchia phase of their work as well.

The angelic alphabet has 21 characters. These showed up for the magicians fully formed with a yellowish tinge in Kelley's vision. Then these letters hovered over a piece of paper and remained visible for a while, giving Kelley enough time to write them out in ink before they faded away.

In angelic language, words are penned from right to left, and that's the same order in which they appeared in Kelley's vision. They were in a single row with dots separating them and a dot before the very first letter as well. The English letters and their angelic translations are as follows:

- B – Pa
- C – veh
- G – ged
- D – gal
- F – or
- A – un
- E – graph
- M – tal
- I – gon
- H – na
- L – ur
- P – mals
- Q – ger

- N – drux
- X – pal
- O – med
- R – don
- Z – ceph
- U – van
- S – fam
- T – gisg

The only letter that has its first letter in caps is Pa. It is very significant in the Heptarchia magic system. For instance, you may have noticed that all 49 good angels' names begin with the letter B (Pa). This same letter shows up a lot on the Ensigns of Creation, and the Holy Table's four corners have oversized Pas as well.

Many commentators have thus come to believe that the letter B must be the same as the number 7, which is the foundational number of these systems. Still, nothing in the actual material suggests that these letters might have specific numerical values. We know for sure that the angel who communicated with Kelley and Dee wanted them to remember all the letters and their names right away. Dee, always the busy bee, had a lot on his plate and didn't want to bother with doing this, but the angel wouldn't let him be. This is clear in the exchange Dee had with the angel Me on March 26, 1583.

Dee: Look, man, I've got a life!

Me: *I instructed thee beforehand and told thee, that both of you must jointly learn those holy letters (Fo, so, I may boldly call them) in memory: with their names: to the intent, that the finger may point to the head and the head to the understanding of his charge.*

Dee: You perceive that I have diverse affairs which at this present do withdraw me from peculiar diligence using to these Characters and their names learning by heart: And therefore, I trust, I shall not offend, if I bestow all the convenient leisure that I shall get, about the learning thereof.

Me: Peace, Thou talkest, as though, thou understandest not. We know there, we see thee in thy heart: Nor one thing shall not let another. For short is the time that shall bring these things to prove.

The Gebofal

The angels had told Kelley and Dee of Gebofal, a great, mystic ritual that would lead to all 49 Gates of Heaven being opened. They would need a series of invocations known as the 49 Keys or Calls to open these gates. These were all communicated to the magicians — except the 49th. The reason they never gave them the final Call was that opening all 49 would lead to the end of days. As the angels wouldn't reveal that final Key, it was a sure thing that the ritual of Gebofal could never be finished in Kelley's or Dee's lifetime. It also meant there would be no apocalyptic consequences as a result of finishing the ritual.

It's easy to assume that the word "apocalypse" is a terrible thing, especially if you've read the book of Revelations in its entirety. However, the word really refers to a revelation of knowledge. We are presently in a New Age, and some would argue it's about time we figured out what the final Key is. Some attempts have been made to discover the missing Key, but there's no way to tell for sure that what they've arrived at is indeed accurate.

Gebofal is the book of Loagaeth in practice. In Dee's journal, the Moon angel Lavanael said:

"Now to work intended, which is called in the Holy Art Gebofal, which is not (as the Philosophers have written) the first step supernatural, but it is the first supernatural step naturally limited unto the 48 Gates of Wisdom, where your holy Book belongeth. The last [Gate] is the speaking with God, as Moses did, which is infinite: All the rest have proper limits, wherein they are contained. But understand that this singular work receiveth Multiplication and dignification, by ascension through all the rest that are limited according to their proper qualities." [A true and Faithful Relation, page 373]

This describes the ritual clearly. It's an ascension through the 49 Gates of Wisdom, which the Tables of Loagaeth represent. Lavanael's description is reminiscent of the Jewish tradition of Counting the Omer and of going through the 50 Gates of *Binah.*

Lavanael says each Gate has proper limits that they are constrained to, and this is most likely because the Tables of the

Holy Book each represent one part of Creation, so the Gate of Wisdom in question would be relegated to that aspect alone. It is just the last Table — which is really the first one — that is infinite and unlimited. Like the Highest Gate of Understanding, this boundless Table is a metaphor for connecting with God directly, just as Moses, who is believed to have passed this Gate when he died.

The Gates of Wisdom (the Tables of Loagaeth) could be considered a form of the Kabbalistic Gates of Understanding. You can find a clue that alludes to this reference in the angel's timing when transmitting the Holy Book — a process that started on March 29, 1583, which was a Good Friday. Good Friday is much like the Jewish Passover, and practically speaking, both events mark the start of Spring. The Passover signified the sparing of the firstborn of the Jewish when the final Plague was sent to wipe out all firstborns of Egypt. This then kicks off the "Counting of the Omer." This is a 50-day period that matches the time of the Israelites Exodus to Mount Sinai, when the initiate or aspirant opens Gates of Understanding and walks right through.

On the Christian end, the Holy or Good Friday is the Crucifixion of Christ. This Friday always comes right before Easter Sunday, which represents the eve of the resurrection of Jesus. This is a three-day period that marks the three days that Christ lay in the tomb, during which he spiritually descended into Hell to do some work, according to various traditions.

Thus, the Angels chose to begin transmitting the Holy Book's text to Dee and Kelley on the Christian festival that most closely correlates to Passover. Then, similar to Counting Omer's fifty-day term, the 48 (actually 49) Tables of Loagaeth were received over forty-eight days. This relationship may serve to explain the Angels' specific observations of magical time throughout receiving Loagaeth, like the following comment from Uriel:

"Behold (sayeth the Lord) I will breathe upon men, and they shall have the spirit of Understanding. In 40 days must the Book of the Secrets, and Key of this World, be written." [Five Books of Mystery]

Another connection between Loagaeth and Counting the Omer is in the Angels' account of the 48 Gates. Dee's Angels prioritized the number 40 and/or 48 over the more customary Jewish fifty days.

As previously stated, Levanael referred to them as the Gates of Wisdom. However, Uriel's phrase in the preceding paragraph refers to the spirit of Binah, which is "the spirit of Understanding." Raphael, the Archangel, also makes a veiled reference to Understanding and the Gates:

"As I have said: the 49 parts of this Book [...] Every element in this mystery is a world of understanding." [Five Books of Mystery]

The Nalvage clarifies this further, according to Dee's journals:

In 49 voices or callings: which are the Natural Keys to open those, not 49 but 48 (for one is not to be opened) Gates of Understanding... [True and Faithful Relation...]

Kabbalistic students will identify Wisdom (Chockmah) as the Supernal Sephiroth's co-equal to Binah. The data presented above indicate that Dee's Angels viewed them as interchangeable. Additionally, there is a cosmic connection between the Jewish version of the Gates and Dee's Version. This is to say that these systems reflect a comparable view of how the cosmos is constructed. Consider the following paragraph from the Sepher ha Zohar, the classic Qabalistic text:

"In that Temple [of Binah], there are 50 gates, which are supposed to be closed, meaning that they block the flow of Lights. There are 49 gates engraved upon the "four winds" of the world. One gate has no direction; it is not known whether it faces up or down. This is how this gate remains closed." [Sepher Zohar, The Locked and the Unlocked, vs. 43ff]

Here, it's clear that the four winds have the 49 Gates engraved on them, representing the four cardinal points. The highest of the gates, however, has no direction of its own. It lies in the middle of the compass.

Additionally, there is a deep relationship between Dee's Heptarchia mysteries and the Loagaeth practice. The evidence of this can be found in the Holy Book, where there are Heptarchic angelic names in the titles and text. Additionally, we should note the Heptarchic Angels — like the Sons and Daughters of Light — revealed many of Loagaeth's mysteries.

Even before Dee and Kelley received this Holy Book, the Archangel Raphael made it abundantly evident that Loagaeth and the Heptarchia were inextricably linked. When he initially exposes the Holy Book to Kelley through the crystal, he expresses unequivocally that it reflects "the measure" of the three magical systems revealed to the two men. (Specifically, the Holy Book, the Heptarchia, and the Earth's Great Table.)

Raphael says:

"This is the Second and the Third: the Third and the last. This is the measure of the whole. (O, what is the man that is worthy of knowing these secrets? Heavy is his wickednesses; mighty is his sin! These shalt thou know. These shall you use. [...] Yet must there be a third, whom God doth not yet choose. The time shall be short, the matter great, the end greater."

Chapter 10: The Enochian Invocations and the Holy Alphabet

The cornerstone of the Enochian magic system is the Invocations (Calls) of Enochian magic. You'll read them in Enochian Language and Dee's English as well. This angelic tongue is very different from the one in the Liber Loagaeth. While they may seem like gibberish, the Calls have been examined, and it's clear that they're written in an actual language, with consistency in definitions, syntax, and grammar.

From April 10, 1584, the first four keys were given to Dee and Kelley, letter by letter. They were delivered backward because the angels had worried that the calls were simply too potent to be delivered straightforwardly. The letters were pulled from various lettered grids. The angels also gave the translations for these calls right after delivering them. But after they were done with the fourth one, they switched things up a bit. It seems they had gotten tired of this tedious delivery method, so they went on to give the magicians calls five through eighteen at once. Then they waited six weeks before giving them the English meanings of each one.

Suppose you think that the translations from the first four keys (which were delivered backward) aligned linguistically with the translations of keys five through eighteen (delivered forward, to be translated six weeks after). In that case, it makes the case that neither Dee nor Kelley just made up the keys or angelic language on their own.

The 18th call is the Call of the Aethyrs or Ayres. The duo received the names of these 30 heavens on July 13, 1584, which was when John Dee turned 57. Before that last communication, the angels gave Dee and his partner an impressive amount of material from April 10 to July 13 to inspire the Golden Dawn adepts to create the hybrid magickal system called Enochian magick. It's a hybrid since Enochian magick was further developed by Crowley and the Golden Dawn and is also based on other ideas that link the 48 calls to other Enochian material that Kelley and Dee got after the keys.

You'll notice that the keys are written like the Biblical psalms, with hard-to-miss poetry. You'll also notice that they're only 48, and that's because the 49th key was withheld from Dee and Kelley to spare humanity the apocalypse. You should pronounce them in Enochian; otherwise, you will not be given access to the Leaves of the Book of Loagaeth.

Quick Pronunciation Guide

All the letters except the ones below are pronounced the same way as in English:

- A is pronounced "ah" as in "mArk'
- C is pronounced "k" as in "Call'
- E is pronounced "eh" as in "grEat'
- I is pronounced "ee" as in "sEE'
- O is pronounced "oh" as in "lOw'
- Q is pronounced "k" as in "Qabbalistic'
- U is pronounced "oo" as in "tOOl'

Enochian Key 1

Ol sonf vorsg, goho Iad balt, lansh calz vonpho: sobra z-ol ror i ta Nazpad Graa ta Malprg Ds hol-q Qaa nothoa zimz Od commah ta nobloh zien: Soba thil gnonp prge aldi Od vrbs oboleh grsam Casarm ohorela caba pir Od zonrensg cab erm Iadnah Pilah farzm zurza adna Ds gono Iadpil Ds hom Od toh Soba Ipam lu Ipamis Ds loholo vep zomd Poamal Od bogpa aai ta piap piamo-i od vaoan ZACARe c-a od ZAMRAM Odo cicle Qaa Zorge, Lap zirdo Noco MAD Hoath Iaida.

In Dee's English: I rayng ouer you, sayeth the God of Iustice, in powre exalted above the firmaments of wrath: in whose hands the Sonne is as a sword and the Mone as a throwgh thrusting fire: which measureth your garments in the mydst of my vestures, and trussed you together as the palms of my hands: whose seats I garnished with the fire of gathering, and bewtified your garments wth admiration. To whome I made a law to govern the holy ones and deliuered you a rod with the ark of knowledg. Moreouer you lifted vp your voyces and sware [obedience and faith to him that liueth and triumpheth] whose begynning is not, nor ende can not be, which shyneth as a flame in the myddst of your pallace, and rayngneth amongst you as the ballance of righteousnes and truth. Moue, therefore, and shew yorselues: open the Mysteries of your Creation: Be frendely vnto me: for I am the servant of the same yor God, the true wurshipper of the Highest.

Enochian Key 2

Adagita vau-pa-ahe zodonugonu fa-a-ipe salada! Vi-i-vau el! Sobame ial-pereji i-zoda-zodazod pi-adapehe casarema aberameji ta ta-labo paracaleda qo-ta lores-el-qo turebesa ooge balatohe! Giui cahisa lusada oreri od micalapape cahisa bia ozodonugonu! lape noanu tarofe coresa tage o-quo maninu IA-I-DON. Torezodu! gohe-el, zodacare eca ca-no-quoda! zodameranu micalazodo od ozodazodame vaurelar; lape zodir IOIAD!Adagita vau-pa-ahe zodonugonu fa-a-ipe salada! Vi-i-vau el! Sobame ial-pereji i-zoda-zodazod pi-adapehe casarema aberameji ta ta-labo paracaleda qo-ta lores-el-qo turebesa ooge balatohe! Giui cahisa lusada oreri od micalapape cahisa bia ozodonugonu! lape noanu tarofe coresa tage o-quo maninu IA-I-DON. Torezodu! gohe-el, zodacare eca ca-no-quoda! zodameranu micalazodo od ozodazodame vaurelar; lape zodir IOIAD!

In Dee's English: Can the wings of the windes vnderstand yor voyces of wunder, O you the second of the first, whome the burning flames haue framed within the depth of my Iaws; whome I haue prepared as Cupps for a Wedding, or as the flowres in their beawty for the Chamber of righteousnes. Stronger are your fete then the barren stone, and mightier are your voices then the manifold windes. For you are become a buylding such as is not, but in the mynde of the All powrefull. Arrise, sayth the First: Move therfore vnto his Servants: Shew your selues in powre: And make me a strong Seething: for I am of him that liueth for euer.

Enochian Key 3

Micma goho Piad zir com-selh a zien biab Os Lon-doh Norz Chis othil Gigipah vnd-l chis ta-pu-im Q mos-pleh teloch Qui-i-n toltorg chis i chis ge m ozien dst brgda od torzul i li F ol balzarg, od aala Thiln Os ne ta ab dluga vomsarg lonsa cap-mi-ali vors cla homil cocasb fafen izizop od mi i noag de gnetaab vaun na-na-e-el panpir Malpirgi caosg Pild noan vnalah balt od vooan do o-i-ap MAD Goholor gohus amiran Micma Iehusoz ca-ca-com od do-o-a-in noar mi-ca-olz a-ai-om Casarmg gohia ZACAR vniglag od Im-ua-mar pugo plapli ananael Q a an.

In Dee's English: Behold, sayeth your god, I am a Circle on whose hands stand 12 Kingdoms: Sis are the seats of Liuing Breath: the rest are as sharp sickles or the horns of death, wherein the Creatures of ye earth are to are not, except myne own hand which slepe and shall ryse. In the first I made you Stuards and placed you in seats 12 of government. giving vnto euery one of you powre successively ouer 456, the true ages of tyme: to the intent that from ye highest vessells and the corners of your governments you might work my powre, powring downe the fires of life and encrease continually on the earth: Thus you are become the skirts of Iustice and Truth. In the Name of the same your God, lift vp, I say, your selues. Behold his mercies florish and Name is become mighty amongst vs. In whome we say: Moue, Descend, and apply your selues vnto vs, as vnto the partakers of the Secret Wisdome of your Creation.

Enochian Key 4

Othil lasdi babge od dorpha Gohol G chis ge auauago cormp pd dsonf vi v-di-v Casarmi oali Map m Sobam ag cormpo c-rp-l Casarmg cro od zi chis od vgeg dst ca pi mali chis ca pi ma on Ionshin chis ta lo Cla Torgu Nor quasahi od F caosaga Bagle zi re nai ad Dsi od Apila Do o a ip Q-a-al ZACAR od ZAMRAN Obelisong rest-el aaf Nor-mo-lap.

In Dee's English: I haue set my fete in the sowth and haue loked abowt me, saying, are not the Thunders of encrease numbred 33 which raigne in the Second Angle? vnder whome I haue placed 9639 whome none hath yet numbred but one, in whome the second beginning of things are and wax strong, which allso successively are the number of time: and their powres are as the first 456. Arrise, you Sonns of pleasure, and viset the earth: for I am the Lord your God which is, and liueth. In the name of the Creator, Move and shew yourselues as pleasant deliuerers, That you may praise him amongst the sonnes of men.

Enochian Key 5

Sa pah zimii du-i-v od noas ta-qu-a-nis adroch dorphal Ca osg od faonts peripsol tablior Casarm amipzi na zarth af od dlugar zizop z-lida caosagi tol torg od z-chis e si asch L ta vi u od iaod thild ds peral hubar Pe o al soba cormfa chis ta la vis od Q-co-casb Ca nils od Darbs Q a as Feth-ar-zi od bliora ia-ial ed nas cicles Bagle Ge iad i L.

In Dee's English: The mighty sownds haue entred in ye 3th Angle and are become as oliues in ye oliue mownt, looking wth gladnes vppon the earth and dwelling in the brightnes of the heuens as contynuall cumforters. vnto whome I fastened pillers of gladnes 19 and gaue them vessels to water the earth wth her creatures: and they are the brothers of the first and second and the beginning of their own sea[ts] which [are garnished with continually burning lamps] 69636 whose numbers are as the first, the endes, and ye contents of tyme. Therfore come you and obey your creation: viset vs in peace and cumfort: Conclude vs as receiuers of yor mysteries: for why? Our Lord and Mr is all One.

Enochian Key 6

Gah s di u chis em micalzo pil zin sobam El harg mir babalon od obloc samvelg dlugar malprg arcaosgi od Acam canal so bol zar f-bliard caosgi od chis a ne tab od miam ta vi v od d Darsar sol peth bi en B ri ta od zacam g mi calzo sob ha hath trian Lu ia he odecrin MAD Q a a on.

In Dee's English: The spirits of ye 4th Angle are Nine, Mighty in the firmament of waters: whome the first hath planted a torment to the wicked and a garland to the righteous: [g]iving vnto them fyrie darts to vanne the earth and 7699 continuall Workmen whose courses viset with cumfort the earth and are in government and contynuance as the second and the third. Wherfore harken vnto my voyce: I haue talked of you and I move you in powre and presence: whose Works shalbe a song of honor and the praise of your God in your Creation.

Enochian Key 7

R a as isalman para di zod oe cri ni aao ial purgah qui in enay butmon od in oas ni para dial casarmg vgear chirlan od zonac Lu cif tian cors to vaul zirn tol ha mi Soba Londoh od miam chis tad o des vmadea od pibliar Othil rit od miam C no quol Rit ZACAR, ZAMRAN oecrimi Q a dah od o mi ca olz aaiom Bagle pap nor id lugam lonshi od vmplif vgegi Bigliad.

In Dee's English: The East is a howse of virgins singing praises amongst the flames of first glory wherein the Lord hath opened his mowth: and they are become 28 liuing dwellings in whome the strength of man reioyseth, and they are apparailed wth ornaments of brightnes such as work wunders on all creatures. Whose Kingdomes and continuance are as the Third and Fowrth Strong Towres and places of cumfort, The seats of Mercy and Continuance. O you Servants of Mercy: Moue, Appeare: sing prayses vnto the Creator and be mighty amongst vs. For to this remembrance is given powre and our strength waxeth strong in our Cumforter.

Enochian Key 8

Bazmelo i ta pi ripson oln Na za vabh ox casarmg vran Chis vgeg dsa bramig bal to ha goho i ad solamian trian ta lol cis A ba i uo nin od a zi agi er rior Ir gil chis da ds pa a ox bufd Caosgo ds chis odi puran teloah cacrg isalman loncho od Vouina carbaf Niiso Bagle auauaga gohon Niiso bagle momao siaion od mabza Iad o i as mo mar poilp Niis ZAMRAN ci a o fi caosgo od bliors od corsi ta a bra mig.

In Dee's English: The Midday, the first, is as the third heaven made of Hiacynet Pillers 26: in whome the Elders are become strong wch I haue prepared for my own righteousnes sayth the Lord: whose long contynuance shall be as bucklers to the stowping Dragon and like vnto the haruest of a Wyddow. How many ar there which remayn in the glorie of the earth, which are, and shall not see death, vntyll this howse fall and the Dragon synck? Come away, for the Thunders haue spoken: Come away, for the Crownes of the Temple and the coat of him that is, was, and shalbe crowned, are diuided. Come, appeare to the terror of the earth and to our comfort and of such as are prepared.

Enochian Key 9

Mica oli bransg prgel napta ialpor ds brin efafafe P vonpho o l a ni od obza Sobca v pa ah chis tatan od tra nan balye a lar lusda so boln od chis hol q C no quo di cial v nal aldon mom caosgo ta las ollor gnay limlal Amma chiis Sobca madrid z chis ooanoan chiis auiny dril pi caosgin od od butmoni parm zum vi C nila Daziz e thamz a-childao od mirc ozol chis pi di a i Collal Vl ci nin a sobam v cim Bagle Iab baltoh chirlan par Niiso od ip ofafafe Bagle acosasb icorsca unig blior.

In Dee's English: A mighty garde of fire wth two edged swords flaming (which haue Viols 8 of Wrath for two tymes and a half: whose wings are of wormwood and of the marrow of salt,) haue stled their feete in the West and are measured with their Ministers 9996. These gather vp the moss of the earth as the rich man doth his threasor: cursed ar they whose iniquities they are in their eyes are milstones greater then the earth, and from their mowthes rune seas of blud: their heds are covered with diamond, and vppon their heds are marble sleus.* Happie is he on whome they frown not. For why? The God of righteousnes reioyseth in them! Come away, and not your Viols, for the tyme is such as requireth cumfort.

Enochian Key 10

Coraxo chis cormp od blans Liucal aziazor paeb soba lilonon chis virq op eophan od salbrox cynixir faboan U nal chis Coust ds saox co casg ol oanio yor eors vohim gizyax od math cocasg plo si molui ds pa ge ip larag om droln matorb cocasb emna L patralx yolci math nomig momons olora gnay angelard Ohio ohio ohio ohio ohio ohio noib ohio caosgon Bagle madrid i zirop chiso drilpa Niiso crip ip nidali.

In Dee's English: The Thunders of Iudgment and Wrath are numbred and are haborowed in the North in the likenes of an oke, whose branches are Nests 22 of Lamentation and Weaping layd vp for the earth, which burn night and day: and vomit out the heds of scorpions and live sulphur myngled with poyson. These be the Thunders that 5678 tymes in ye 24th part of a moment rore [with a hundred mighty earthquakes and a thousand] tymes as many surges. which rest not neyther know any echoing* tyme here. One rock bringeth furth 1000, euen as the hart of man doth his thowghts. Wo, Wo, Wo, Wo, Wo, Wo, yea Wo be to the earth! For her iniquitie is, was and shalbe great! Come awaye: but not your noyses. (* "Any echoing time between.")

Enochian Key 11

Ox i ay al holdo od zirom O Coraxo ds zddar ra asy od vab zir comliax od ba hal Niiso salman teloch Casar man holq od ti ta z-chis soba cormf i ga Niisa Bagle abramg noncp ZACARe ca od ZAMRAN odo cicle qaa Zorge lap zirdo noco Mad Hoath Iaida.

In Dee's English: The Mighty Seat groaned and they were 5 thunders which flew into the East: and the Egle spake and cryed wth a lowde voyce, Come awaye: [and they gathered themselues together and became] the howse of death of whome it is measured and it is as they are, whose number is 31. Come away, for I haue prepared for you. Moue therfore, and shew your selues: open the Mysteries of your Creation: be frendely vnto me: for I am the servant of ye same yor God, the true wurshipper of the Highest.

Enochian Key 12

Nonci dsonf Babage od chis ob hubaio tibibp allar atraah od ef drix fafen Mian ar E nay ovof soba do o a in aai i VONPH ZACAR gohus od ZAMRAM odo cicle Qaa Zorge, lap zirdo noco MAD Hoath Iaida.

In Dee's English: O you that rayng in the Sowth and are 28, The Lanterns of Sorrow, bynde vp yor girdles and viset vs. Bring down your trayn 3663 that the Lord may be magnified, whose name amongst you is Wrath. Moue, I say, and shew yor selues: open ye Mysteries of yor Creation: be frendely vnto me: for I am the servant of the same yor God, the true wurshipper of the Highest.

Enochian Key 13

Napeai Babgen ds brin vx ooaona lring vonph doalim eolis ollog orsba ds chis affa Micma isro MAD od Lonshitox ds ivmd aai GROSB ZACAR od ZAMRAN, odo cicle Qaa, zorge, lap zirdo noco MAD Hoath Iaida.

In Dee's English: O you swords of the Sowth which haue 42 eyes to styr vp the wrath of synn, making men drunken which are empty.

Behold the promise of God and his powre which is called amongst you a Bitter Sting. Moue and shew your selues: open the Mysteryes of yor Creation: be frendly vnto me: for I am the servant of ye same yor God, the true wurshipper of the Highest.

Enochian Key 14

Noromi bagie pasbs oiad ds trint mirc ol thil dods tolham caosgo Ho min ds brin oroch Quar Micma bial oiad a is ro tox dsi vm aai Baltim ZACAR od ZAMRAN odo cicle Qaa, zorge, lap zirdo noco MAD, hoath Iaida.

In Dee's English: O you sonns of fury, the dowghters of the lust, which sit vppon 24 seats, vexing all creatures of the earth with age, which haue vnder you 1636: behold the Voyce of God, the promys of him which is called amongst you Furye or Extreme Iustice. Moue and shew yor selues: open the Mysteries of yor Creation: be frendely vnto me: for I am the servant of the same your God, the true wurshipper of the Highest.

Enochian Key 15

Ils tabaan li al prt casarman Vpahi chis darg dso ado caosgi orscor ds omax nonasci Baeouib od emetgis iaiadix ZACAR od ZAMRAN, odo cicle Qaa, zorge, lap zirdo noco MAD, hoath Iaida.

In Dee's English: O thow the governor of the first flame vnder whose wyngs are 6739 which weaue the earth wth drynes: which knowest the great name Righteousnes and the Seale of Honor. Moue and shew yor selues: open the Mysteries of yor Creation: be frendely vnto me: for I am the servant of the same your God, the true wurshipper of the High[e]st.

Enochian Key 16

Ils viuialprt salman blat ds acro odzi busd od bliorax balit dsin-si caosg lusdan Emod dsom od tli-ob drilpa geh uls MAD zilodarp ZACAR od ZAMRAN odo cicle Qaa, zorge, lap zirdo noco MAD, hoath Iaida.

In Dee's English: O thow second flame, the howse of Iustice, which hast thy begynning in glory and shalt cumfort the iust: which walkest on the eart[h] with feete 8763 that vnderstand and separate creatures: great art thow in the God of Stretch Furth and Conquere. Moue and shew yor selues: open the Mysteries of yor Creation: be frendely vnto me: for I am the servant of the same your God, the true wurshipper of the Highest.

Enochian Key 17

Ils do alprt soba vpa ah chis manba zixlay dodshi od brint Taxs hubaro tas tax ylsi, so bai ad I von po vnph Aldon dax il od toatar ZACAR od ZAMRAN odo cicle Qaa zorge lap zirdo Noco MAD hoath Iaida.

In Dee's English: O thow third flame whose wyngs are thorns to styr vp vexation and hast 7336 Lamps Liuing going before the[e], whose God is Wrath in Angre, gyrd vp thy loynes and harken. Moue and shew yor selues: open the Mysteries of yor Creation: be frendely vnto me: for I am the servant of the same your God, the true wurshipper of the Highest.

Enochian Key 18

Ils Micail-z olprit ial prg Bliors ds odo Cusdir oiad o uo ars caosgo Ca sar mg La iad eran brints cafafam ds iumd a q lo a do hi MOZ od ma of fas Bolp comobliort pambt ZACAR od ZAMRAN odo cicle Qaa zorge lap zirdo Noco MAD, hoath Iaida.

In Dee's English: O thow mighty Light and burning flame of cumfort which openest the glory of God to the center of the erth, in whome the Secrets of Truth 6332 haue their abiding, which is called in thy kingdome Ioye and not to be measured: be thow a wyndow of cumfort vnto me. Moue and shew your selues: open the Mysteries of your Creation: be frendely vnto me: for I am the servant of the same your God, the true wurshipper of the Highest.

The Key or Call of the 30 Aethyrs

These are 30 Aethyrs names:

       1) LIL
       2) ARN
       3) ZOM
       4) PAZ
       5) LAT
       6) MAZ
       7) DEO
       8) ZID
       9) ZIP

10) ZAX
11) ICH
12) LOW
13) ZIM
14) VTA
15) OXO
16) LEA
17) TAN
18) ZEN
19) POP
20) CHR
21) ASP
22) LIN
23) TOR
24) NIA
25) VTI
26) DES
27) ZAA
28) BAG
29) RII
30) TEX

The Enochian Call of the 30 Aethyrs

Madriax ds praf {Name of Aether, eg LIL} chis Micaolz saanir caosgo od fisis bal zizras Iaida nonca gohulim Micma adoian MAD I a od Bliorb sa ba ooaona chis Luciftias peripsol ds abraassa noncf netaa ib caosgi od tilb adphaht dam ploz tooat noncf gmi calzoma L rasd tofglo marb yarry I DOI GO od tor zulp ia o daf gohol caosga ta ba ord saanir od christeos yr poil ti ob l Bus dir tilb noaln pa id orsba od dodrmni zylna El zap tilb parm gi pe rip sax od ta qurlst bo o a pi S L nib m ov cho symp od Christeos Ag tol torn mirc q ti ob l Lel, Tom paombd dilzmo aspian, Od christeos Ag L tor torn parach a symp, Cord ziz dod pal od fifalz L s mnad od fargt bams omaoas Conisbra od auauox tonug Ors cat bl noasmi tab ges Leuith mong vnchi omp tilb ors. Bagle Mo o o ah ol cord ziz L ca pi ma o ix o maxip od ca co casb gsaa Baglen pi i tianta a ba ba lond od faorgt teloc vo v im Ma dri iax tirzu o adriax oro cha aboapri Tabaori priaz ar ta bas. A dr pan cor sta dobix Yol cam pri a zi ar coazior. Od quasb q ting Ripir pa a oxt sa ga cor. vm l od prd zar ca crg A oi ve a e cormpt TORZV ZACAR od ZAMRAN aspt sibsi but mona ds surzas tia baltan ODO cicle Qaa Od Ozama plapli Iad na mad.

In Dee's English: O you heuens which dwell in the First Ayre, the mightie in the partes of the Erth, and execute the Iudgment of the Highest! To you it is sayd, Beholde the face of your God, the begynning of cumfort, whose eyes are the brightnes of the hevens: which prouided you for the gouernment of the Erth and her vnspeakable varietie, furnishing you wth a powr vnderstand to dispose all things according to the providence of Him that sitteth on the Holy Throne, and rose vp in the begynning, saying: the Earth let her be gouerned by her parts and let there be diuision in her, that the glory of hir may be allwayes drunken and vexed in it self. Her course, let it ronne wth the hevens, and as a handmayd let her serve them. One season let it confownd an other, and let there be no creature vppon or within her the same: all her members let them differ in their qualities, and let there be no one creature aequall wth an other: the reasonable Creatures of the Erth let them vex and weede out one an other, and the dwelling places let them forget thier names: the work of man, and his pomp, let them be defaced: his buyldings let them become caves for the beasts of the feeld. Confownd her vnderstanding with darknes. For why? It repenteth me I made Man. One while let her be known and an other while a stranger: bycause she is the bed of a Harlot, and the dwelling place of Him that is Faln. O you heuens arrise: the lower heuens vnder neath you, let them serve you! Gouern those that govern: cast down such as fall! Bring furth with those that encrease, and destroy the rotten! No place let it remayne in one number: ad and diminish vntill the stars be numbred!

Arrise, Move, and Appere before the Couenant of his mowth, which he hath sworne vnto vs in his Iustice. Open the Mysteries of your Creation: and make vs partakers of Vndefyled Knowledg.

The Round Tablet of Nalvage

The Round Tablet of Nalvage is anything but round. It's a square split into four more squares (also called continents), with four outer bars around it. The bars and continents are further split into lettered squares, so that each continent has nine squares, and each bar has four. Angel Nalvage had told Kelley and Dee that the first two continents, 1 and 2 (on the left-hand side) were "dignified." Continents 3 was "not yet dignified, but to be dignified," and continent 4 was "without glory or dignity." Nalvage went on to describe these continents in Latin:

> 1) Continent 1: *Vita suprema,* which means "highest life." This is also the "continent of joy."
>
> 2) Continent 2: *Vita,* meaning "life." This is the "continent of potentiality."
>
> 3) Continent 3: *Vita non dignificata, sed dignificanda,* meaning, "life not dignified, but which shall be dignified." This is the continent of "creation."
>
> 4) Continent 4: *Vita est etiam haec, sed quae perperit mors,* meaning "Even this is life, but life which will be paid with death." This is the "continent of discord."

Each continent of the round table has nine letters that you can read in different ways to create actual words in the angelic language. When you read it counterclockwise, the tablet's outer bars will spell out the names of the four kinds of angels:

- The Luah (praising angels)

- The Lang (ministering angels)

- The Sach (confirming angels)

- The Urch (confounding angels)

These angels limit the work of the angelic forces in each continent, keeping them contained. Nalvage then offered the Latin interpretations of the words within the continents when you read them from left to right as follows:

- Idz — Gaudium — Joy

- Aoi — Praesentia — Presence

- Mzr — Laudentes — Praising

- Sai — Actio — Action
- God — Factum — Events
- Urr — Confirmantes — Establishing
- Bna — Protestas — Power
- Daz — Motus — Motion
- Iab — Ministrantes — Ministering
- Fos — Luctos — Lamentation
- Sea — Discordia — Discord
- Rdi — Confundantes — Confusing

The outer corners of each continent spell out *iad*, the Enochian word that means God. The three letters running diagonally spell *moz* (joy), *sor* (action), *bab* (power), and ser (lamentation). Then you have the three letters of the continents' inner corners spelling out *zir* (I am), *zna* (motion), *osf* (discord), and *gru* (deed). Putting these words together, you can create phrases like these:

Continent 4: God's Discord and Lamentation (*iad ser osf*)

Continent 3: Result of God's Action (*iad sor gru*)

Continent 2: God's Power in Motion (*iad bab zna*)

Continent 1: I am the Joy if God (iad moz zir)

Nalvage said that as far as the entire tablet is concerned, "the Substance is attributed to God the Father." Speaking of the outer bars' letters, he said, "The first circular mover, the circumference, God the Son, The Finger of the Gather, and Mover of all things." On the continents and how their letters should be read, he said, "The order and knitting together of the parts in their due and perfect proportion, God the Holy Ghost. Lo the beginning and end of all things."

When the Round Tablet of Nalvage is decoded, it shows angelic and divine names and words that are always in motion, in a way that is reminiscent of a choir of angels. It's not clear if Nalvage went on to disclose how the tablet should be used. However, it's clear that the magicians Kelley and Dee had gotten what was left of the Enochian magick system 90 days or less after receiving this tablet. This makes some historians and magicians wonder if the Round Tablet might have been the catalyst or if it was the key to an unexpressed "first call," if not the call itself.

Chapter 11: The Parts of the Earth and the 30 Aethyrs

Dee was very interested in the political happenings in Poland and had really wanted to get information from the angels. Nalvage had tried to explain to him how spirits are in charge of various parts of the earth. In the process, he explained how everything, both in heaven and on earth, is connected to everything else. Dee noted all that the angel had revealed to him about this in the *Liber Scientae Auxilii et Vitoriae Terrestris.*

Nalvage began by splitting the universe into 30 parts that would later become known as Aethyrs or Aires. He assigned 91 parts of the earth to the 30 Aires. At first, he referred to locations around the earth by the names known to Dee and Kelley and then by their divine names. Then he assigned each of the tribes of Israel these name pairs, along with their angelic king, ministers, and coordinates. Please note that the following are listed sequentially.

Aire Number 1, Ruled by LIL

Part of the Earth: Aegyptus

Divine Name: Occodon

Tribe: Neftalim

Quarter of Earth: East N-E

Angelic Kind: Zarzlig

Number of good ministers: 7209
Part of the Earth: Syria
Divine Name: Pascomb
Tribe: Zabulon
Quarter of Earth: West S-W
Angelic Kind: Zinggen
Number of good ministers: 2360
Name of good princes of the Air:
Part of the Earth: Mesopotamia
Divine Name: Valgars
Tribe: Izachar
Quarter of Earth: West N-W
Angelic Kind: Alpudus
Number of good ministers: 5362

Aire Number 2, Ruled by ARN

Part of the Earth: Cappadocia
Divine Name: Doagnis
Tribe: Manasses
Quarter of Earth: North
Angelic Kind: Zarnaah
Number of good ministers: 3636
Part of the Earth: Ertruria
Divine Name: Pacasna
Tribe: Reuben
Quarter of Earth: South
Angelic Kind: Ziracah
Number of good ministers: 2362
Part of the Earth: Asia Minor
Divine Name: Dialioa
Tribe: Reuben
Quarter of Earth: South
Angelic Kind: Ziracah

Number of good ministers: 8962

Aire Number 3, Ruled by ZOM

Part of the Earth: Hyrcania

Divine Name: Samapha

Tribe: Neftalim

Quarter of Earth: East N-E

Angelic Kind: Zarzlig

Number of good ministers: 4400

Part of the Earth: Thracia

Divine Name: Virooli

Tribe: Izachar

Quarter of Earth: West N-W

Angelic Kind: Alpudus

Number of good ministers: 3660

Part of the Earth: Gosmam

Divine Name: Andispi

Tribe: Gad

Quarter of Earth: South S-E

Angelic Kind: Lavavot

Number of good ministers: 9236

Aire Number 4, Ruled by PAZ

Part of the Earth: Thebaidi

Divine Name: Thotanp

Tribe: Gad

Quarter of Earth: South S-E

Angelic Kind: Lavavot

Number of good ministers: 2360

Part of the Earth: Parsadal

Divine Name: Axziarg

Tribe: Gad

Quarter of Earth: South S-E

Angelic Kind: Lavavot

Number of good ministers: 3000
Part of the Earth: India
Divine Name: Pothnir
Tribe: Efraim
Quarter of Earth: North N-W
Angelic Kind: Arfaolg
Number of good ministers: 6300

Aire Number 5, Ruled by LIT

Part of the Earth: Bactriane
Divine Name: Lazdixi
Tribe: Dan
Quarter of Earth: East
Angelic Kind: Olpaged
Number of good ministers: 8630
Part of the Earth: Cilicia
Divine Name: Nocamal
Tribe: Izachar
Quarter of Earth: West N-W
Angelic Kind: Alpudus
Number of good ministers: 2306
Part of the Earth: Oxiana
Divine Name: Tiarpax
Tribe: Zabulon
Quarter of Earth: West S-W
Angelic Kind: Zinggen
Number of good ministers: 5802

Aire Number 6, Ruled by MAZ

Part of the Earth: Numidia
Divine Name: Saxtomp
Tribe: Asser
Quarter of Earth: East S-E
Angelic Kind: Gebabal

Number of good ministers: 3620
Part of the Earth: Cyprus
Divine Name: Vavaamp
Tribe: Efraim
Quarter of Earth: North N-W
Angelic Kind: Arfaolg
Number of good ministers: 9200
Part of the Earth: Parthia
Divine Name: Zirzird
Tribe: Asser
Quarter of Earth: East S-E
Angelic Kind: Gebabal
Number of good ministers: 7720

Aire Number 7, Ruled by DEO
Part of the Earth: Getulia
Divine Name: Opmacas
Tribe: Manasses
Quarter of Earth: North
Angelic Kind: Zarnaah
Number of good ministers: 6363
Part of the Earth: Arabia
Divine Name: Genadol
Tribe: Judah
Quarter of Earth: West
Angelic Kind: Homonol
Number of good ministers: 7706
Part of the Earth: Phalagon
Divine Name: Aspiaon
Tribe: Zabulon
Quarter of Earth: West S-W
Angelic Kind: Zinggen
Number of good ministers: 6320

Aire Number 8, Ruled by ZID

Part of the Earth: Mantiana

Divine Name: Zamfres

Tribe: Asser

Quarter of Earth: East S-E

Angelic Kind: Gebabal

Number of good ministers: 4362

Part of the Earth: Soxia

Divine Name: Todnaon

Tribe: Dan

Quarter of Earth: East

Angelic Kind: Olpaged

Number of good ministers: 7236

Part of the Earth: Gallia

Divine Name: Pristac

Tribe: Neftalim

Quarter of Earth: East N-E

Angelic Kind: Zarzilg

Number of good ministers: 2302

Aire Number 9, Ruled by ZIP

Part of the Earth: Assyria

Divine Name: Oddiorg

Tribe: Judah

Quarter of Earth: West

Angelic Kind: Hononol

Number of good ministers: 9996

Part of the Earth: Sogdiana

Divine Name: Cralpir

Tribe: Gad

Quarter of Earth: South S-E

Angelic Kind: Lavavot

Number of good ministers: 3620

Part of the Earth: Lydia
Divine Name: Doanzin
Tribe: Neftalim
Quarter of Earth: East N-E
Angelic Kind: Zarzilg
Number of good ministers: 4230
Aire Number 10, Ruled by ZAX
Part of the Earth: Caspis
Divine Name: Lexarph
Tribe: Zabulon
Quarter of Earth: West S-W
Angelic Kind: Zinggen
Number of good ministers: 8880
Part of the Earth: Germania
Divine Name: Comanan
Tribe: Izachar
Quarter of Earth: West N-W
Angelic Kind: Alpudus
Number of good ministers: 1230
Part of the Earth: Trenam
Divine Name: Tabitom
Tribe: Neftalim
Quarter of Earth: East N-E
Angelic Kind: Zarzilg
Number of good ministers: 1617
Aire Number 11, Ruled by ICH
Part of the Earth: Bithynia
Divine Name: Molpand
Tribe: Gad
Quarter of Earth: South S-E
Angelic Kind: Lavavot
Number of good ministers: 3472

Part of the Earth: Gracia
Divine Name: Usnarda
Tribe: Simeon
Quarter of Earth: South S-W
Angelic Kind: Zurchol
Number of good ministers: 7236
Part of the Earth: Licia
Divine Name: Ponodol
Tribe: Juda
Quarter of Earth: West
Angelic Kind: Hononol
Number of good ministers: 5234
Aire Number 12, Ruled by LOE
Part of the Earth: Onigap
Divine Name: Tapamal
Tribe: Simeon
Quarter of Earth: South S-W
Angelic Kind: Zurchol
Number of good ministers: 2658
Part of the Earth: India Major
Divine Name: Gedoons
Tribe: Benjamin
Quarter of Earth: North N-E
Angelic Kind: Cadaamp
Number of good ministers: 7772
Part of the Earth: Orchenii
Divine Name: Ambriol
Tribe: Reuben
Quarter of Earth: South
Angelic Kind: Ziracah
Number of good ministers: 3391

Aire Number 13, Ruled by ZIM

Part of the Earth: Achaia
Divine Name: Gecaond
Tribe: Gad
Quarter of Earth: South S-E
Angelic Kind: Lavavot
Number of good ministers: 8111
Part of the Earth: Armenia
Divine Name: Laparin
Tribe: Dan
Quarter of Earth: East
Angelic Kind: Olpaged
Number of good ministers: 336
Part of the Earth: Nemrodiana
Divine Name: Docepax
Tribe: Izachar
Quarter of Earth: West N-W
Angelic Kind: Alpudus
Number of good ministers: 4213

Aire Number 14, Ruled by VTA

Part of the Earth: Paphlagonia
Divine Name: Tedoond
Tribe: Asser
Quarter of Earth: East S-E
Angelic Kind: Gebabal
Number of good ministers: 2673
Part of the Earth: Phasiana
Divine Name: Vivipos
Tribe: Izachar
Quarter of Earth: West N-W
Angelic Kind: Alpudus
Number of good ministers: 8230

Part of the Earth: Chaldei
Divine Name: Ooanamb
Tribe: Efraim
Quarter of Earth: North N-W
Angelic Kind: Arfaolg
Number of good ministers: 8230

Aire Number 15, Ruled by OXO

Part of the Earth: Itergi
Divine Name: Tahamdo
Tribe: Neftalim
Quarter of Earth: East N-E
Angelic Kind: Zirzilg
Number of good ministers: 1367
Part of the Earth: Macedonia
Divine Name: Nociabi
Tribe: Gad
Quarter of Earth: South S-E
Angelic Kind: Lavavot
Number of good ministers: 1367
Part of the Earth: Garamantica
Divine Name: Tastoxo
Tribe: Efraim
Quarter of Earth: North N-W
Angelic Kind: Arfaolg
Number of good ministers: 1886

Aire Number 16, Ruled by LEA

Part of the Earth: Saoromatica
Divine Name: Cucarpt
Tribe: Reuben
Quarter of Earth: South
Angelic Kind: Ziracah
Number of good ministers: 9920

Part of the Earth: Aethiopia
Divine Name: Lavacon
Tribe: Judah
Quarter of Earth: West
Angelic Kind: Honolol
Number of good ministers: 9230
Part of the Earth: Fiacins
Divine Name: Sochial
Tribe: Efraim
Quarter of Earth: North N-W
Angelic Kind: Arfaolg
Number of good ministers: 9240

Aire Number 17, Ruled by TAN

Part of the Earth: Cholchica
Divine Name: Sigmorf
Tribe: Reuben
Quarter of Earth: South
Angelic Kind: Zirnesh
Number of good ministers: 9623
Part of the Earth: Coreniaca
Divine Name: Aydropt
Tribe: Dan
Quarter of Earth: East
Angelic Kind: Olpaged
Number of good ministers: 9132
Part of the Earth: Nasamonia
Divine Name: Torcazi
Tribe: Neftalim
Quarter of Earth: East N-E
Angelic Kind: Zirzilg
Number of good ministers: 2634

Aire Number 18, Ruled by ZEN

Part of the Earth: Carthago
Divine Name: Nabaomi
Tribe: Asser
Quarter of Earth: East S-E
Angelic Kind: Gebebal
Number of good ministers: 2346
Part of the Earth: Coxlant
Divine Name: Zafasai
Tribe: Izachar
Quarter of Earth: West N-W
Angelic Kind: Alpudus
Number of good ministers: 9276
Part of the Earth: Idumea
Divine Name: Yalpamb
Tribe: Efraim
Quarter of Earth: West N-W
Angelic Kind: Alpudus
Number of good ministers: 2689

Aire Number 19, Ruled by POP

Part of the Earth: Parstavia
Divine Name: Torzoxi
Tribe: Efraim
Quarter of Earth: North N-W
Angelic Kind: Arfaolg
Number of good ministers: 6236
Part of the Earth: Celtica
Divine Name: Abaiond
Tribe: Benjamin
Quarter of Earth: North N-E
Angelic Kind: Cadaamp
Number of good ministers: 6732

Part of the Earth: Vinsan
Divine Name: Omagrap
Tribe: Zabulon
Quarter of Earth: West S-W
Angelic Kind: Zinggen
Number of good ministers: 2388

Aire Number 20, Ruled by CHR
Part of the Earth: Tolpan
Divine Name: Zildron
Tribe: Asser
Quarter of Earth: East S-E
Angelic Kind: Gebabal
Number of good ministers: 3626
Part of the Earth: Carcedonia
Divine Name: Parziba
Tribe: Judah
Quarter of Earth: West
Angelic Kind: Hononol
Number of good ministers: 7629
Part of the Earth: Italia
Divine Name: Totocan
Tribe: Izachar
Quarter of Earth: West N-W
Angelic Kind: Alpudus
Number of good ministers: 3634

Aire Number 21, Ruled by ASP
Part of the Earth: Brytania
Divine Name: Chirspa
Tribe: Efraim
Quarter of Earth: North N-W
Angelic Kind: Arfaolg
Number of good ministers: 5536

Part of the Earth: Phenices
Divine Name: Toantom
Tribe: Benjamin
Quarter of Earth: North N-E
Angelic Kind: Cedaamp
Number of good ministers: 5635
Part of the Earth: Comaginen
Divine Name: Vixpalg
Tribe: Simeon
Quarter of Earth: South S-W
Angelic Kind: Zurchol
Number of good ministers: 5658

Aire Number 22, Ruled by LIN

Part of the Earth: Apulia
Divine Name: Ozidain
Tribe: Afraim
Quarter of Earth: North N-W
Angelic Kind: Arfaolg
Number of good ministers: 2232
Part of the Earth: Marmarica
Divine Name: Paraoan
Tribe: Dan
Quarter of Earth: East
Angelic Kind: Olpaged
Number of good ministers: 2326
Part of the Earth: Concava Syria
Divine Name: Calzirg
Tribe: Efraim
Quarter of Earth: North N-W
Angelic Kind: Arfaolg
Number of good ministers: 2367

Aire Number 23, Ruled by TOR

Part of the Earth: Gebal
Divine Name: Ronoamb
Tribe: Manasseh
Quarter of Earth: North
Angelic Kind: Zarnaah
Number of good ministers: 7320
Part of the Earth: Elam
Divine Name: Onizimp
Tribe: Gad
Quarter of Earth: South S-E
Angelic Kind: Lavavot
Number of good ministers: 7262
Part of the Earth: Idunia
Divine Name: Zaxanin
Tribe: Zabulon
Quarter of Earth: West S-W
Angelic Kind: Zinggen
Number of good ministers: 7333

Aire Number 24, Ruled by NIA

Part of the Earth: Media
Divine Name: Orcanir
Tribe: Mannaseh
Quarter of Earth: North
Angelic Kind: Zarnaah
Number of good ministers: 8200
Part of the Earth: Ariana
Divine Name: Chialps
Tribe: Gad
Quarter of Earth: South S-E
Angelic Kind: Lavavot
Number of good ministers: 8350

Part of the Earth: Chaldea
Divine Name: Soageel
Tribe: Zabulon
Quarter of Earth: West S-W
Angelic Kind: Zinggen
Number of good ministers: 8236

Aire Number 25, Ruled by UTI

Part of the Earth: Sericipopuli
Divine Name: Mirzind
Tribe: Manasseh
Quarter of Earth: North
Angelic Kind: Zarnaah
Number of good ministers: 5632

Part of the Earth: Persia
Divine Name: Obuaors
Tribe: Reuben
Quarter of Earth: South
Angelic Kind: Ziracah
Number of good ministers: 6333

Part of the Earth: Gongatha
Divine Name: Ranglam
Tribe: Efraim
Quarter of Earth: North N-W
Angelic Kind: Arfaolg
Number of good ministers: 9232

Aire Number 26, Ruled by DES

Part of the Earth: Gorsim
Divine Name: Pophand
Tribe: Efraim
Quarter of Earth: North N-W
Angelic Kind: Arfaolg
Number of good ministers: 9232

Part of the Earth: Hispania
Divine Name: Nigrana
Tribe: Benjamin
Quarter of Earth: North N-E
Angelic Kind: Cadaamp
Number of good ministers: 3637
Part of the Earth: Pamphilia
Divine Name: Bazchim
Tribe: Efraim
Quarter of Earth: North N-W
Angelic Kind: Arfaolg
Number of good ministers: 3637

Aire Number 27, Ruled by ZAA

Part of the Earth: Occidi
Divine Name: Saziami
Tribe: Reuben
Quarter of Earth: South
Angelic Kind: Ziracah
Number of good ministers: 7220
Part of the Earth: Babylon
Divine Name: Mathula
Tribe: Manasseh
Quarter of Earth: North
Angelic Kind: Zarnash
Number of good ministers: 7560
Part of the Earth: Median
Divine Name: Orpanib
Tribe: Asser
Quarter of Earth: East S-E
Angelic Kind: Gebabal
Number of good ministers: 7263

Aire Number 28, Ruled by BAG

Part of the Earth: Idumian
Divine Name: Labnixp
Tribe: Gad
Quarter of Earth: South S-W
Angelic Kind: Lavavot
Number of good ministers: 2630
Part of the Earth: Felix Arabia
Divine Name: Cocisni
Tribe: Neftalim
Quarter of Earth: East N-E
Angelic Kind: Zarzilg
Number of good ministers: 7236
Part of the Earth: Metfonitidim
Divine Name: Oxlopar
Tribe: Simeon
Quarter of Earth: South S-W
Angelic Kind: Zurchol
Number of good ministers: 8200

Aire Number 29, Ruled by RII

Part of the Earth: Assyria
Divine Name: Vastrim
Tribe: Judah
Quarter of Earth: West
Angelic Kind: Honolol
Number of good ministers: 9632
Part of the Earth: Affrica
Divine Name: Odraxti
Tribe: Manasse
Quarter of Earth: North
Angelic Kind: Zaenaah
Number of good ministers: 4236

Part of the Earth: Bactriani
Divine Name: Comziam
Tribe: Efraim
Quarter of Earth: North N-W
Angelic Kind: Arfaolg
Number of good ministers: 7635

Aire Number 30, Ruled by TEX

Part of the Earth: Phrygia
Divine Name: Gemnimb
Tribe: Manasseh
Quarter of Earth: North
Angelic Kind: Zarnaah
Number of good ministers: 9636
Part of the Earth: Creta
Divine Name: Advorpt
Tribe: Judah
Quarter of Earth: West
Angelic Kind: Honolol
Number of good ministers: 7632
Part of the Earth: Mauritania
Divine Name: Dozinal
Tribe: Simeon
Quarter of Earth: South S-W
Angelic Kind: Zurchol
Number of good ministers: 5632

To be clear, these parts aren't the same as the "governors of the Aethyrs." It doesn't refer to any specific spiritual being but the locale of the world of Enochian magic, which has its own qualities. Also, the Parts do not rule the Aethyr, as they are only portions of the latter. You can think of the connection between the two as being like the relationship between the zodiac signs and decanates, which are only a section of the signs. Also, the Voice of the Part isn't considered a Part itself but as an unnamed minister who dwells within. Following are Zodiac signs, their kings, and their respective tribes:

Aries: King Alpudus, Isacarah

Taurus: King Honolol, Iehudah

Gemini: King Zarzilg, Nephthalim

Cancer: King Gebabal, Asseir

Leo: King Olpaged, Dan

Virgo: King Cadaamp, Benjamin

Libra: King Zarnaah, Manasse

Scorpio: King Arfaolg, Ephraim

Capricorn: King Zurchol, Simeon

Aquarius: King Ziracah, Ruben

Pisces: King Zinggen, Zabulon

The idea behind this system is based on the Tribes' disposition, as shown in the book of Numbers Chapter 2, along with Dee's drawing of it. There are several systems you can get using these sources. Some visions line up with their corresponding attributes, while others only minimally factor in it, and others are completely out of sync with it. Note that all 12 signs of the Zodiac are governed by the same angels in charge of the Aires. Clearly, the angels can ignore the traits whenever they deem it fit.

The Watchtowers

The Great Table has four smaller ones that represent the four classical elements and the four directions. Each is a Watchtower that has a Great King. Seniors, angels, and demons also accompany this King. The four Watchtowers guard the material world and maintain it, making sure it runs as it should. They are connected by the 5th Element, represented by the Black Cross.

Each Watchtower has 13 rows and 12 columns of letters, totaling 156 letters each. Some are in lowercase, while the rest are in uppercase, and two letters in each Watchtower are set backward. Each one is further split into four quadrants by another cross formed by the 6th and 7th columns and the 7th row. These quadrants consist of 6 rows and 5 columns.

You'll find a cross created by the 2nd row and 3rd column of the quadrant in question in each quadrant. The Black Cross only carries four names, but the bottom and left of the cross reflect the names. The angels had told Dee to write the letters of the Great Table in English, not the celestial tongue. This is important as the Angelic Script has neither lower nor uppercase letters. Dee and Kelley created the grid and lettered the hundreds of squares, writing the capitals at somewhat random locations. There is no discernible reason that there are eight letters written backward, and the angels wouldn't give an answer for that choice. It wasn't until many years after the sessions were over and Kelley had moved on that Dee finally figured it out.

The capitals were the initial letters of the names of the Governors. These names make up the Great Table's letters, with each one arranged to match its sigil's shape, like the pieces of a puzzle. So, the Watchtowers serve as a mirror of the Heavens above, consisting of 22 Governors. The reversed letters are a different matter. There's an L that circles back around to the Watchtower's Black Cross, creating the name of a Governor. This leaves PARAON curiously unaccounted for. Naturally, Dee asked about this, and the angels warned that every letter was living fire. They also said that the final N was very destructive.

What is important about the 91 parts of the earth and the 30 Aethyrs is that it demonstrates the divine connection between all levels of consciousness. As such, the Great Table shows how all things in heaven and earth are connected.

Conclusion

It must seem fairly obvious that there is so much depth to the mystical art of Enochian magic. This is a very potent form of magic you can utilize if you – like John Dee – would like to connect with the angels and learn the universe's secrets.

Many would discredit the wisdom and wonder of Enochian magic, either by pointing out Kelley's shady past or simply deciding that Dee was a brilliant mind who dabbled in things he shouldn't have and then went off the deep end. This is absolutely not the case. Further study of Enochian magic will show you that what you've learned so far has been nothing short of the work of divinity itself.

To take advantage of this form of magic, the magician must first understand that magic will not work unless and until they accept that it is valid and that the power lies within them. Being even more potent than any other form of magic, Enochian magic will give you the tools to connect with the divine and then ask infinite and wise beings how you can make your life better or get closer to fulfilling your purpose in life. What could be better than receiving direct, divine counsel straight from the lips of angels?

The trouble with religion and society is that everyone seeks answers, but they're asking all the wrong questions and seeking answers from all the wrong places. Searching for things on the internet can only get you so far. Seeking answers to life's tough questions from "spiritual gurus" can only satisfy you so much.

Getting these answers from the ones who know the being that created you is *where it's at!*

In conclusion, your journey has only begun. See what the great Aleister Crowley has to say about this wonderful form of magic. If you practice this form of magic seriously, then you can't just stop at reading. You must act on what you now know, and even better, study other literature on the topic. Read the works of Dee and Kelley. As you learn and practice, you will come to know things that no book, no guru, no guide could ever teach you. All you have to do is be proactive about deepening your practice, and you'll develop a richer, fuller, more satisfying life. It's up to you to determine how deep into the rabbit hole you want to go.

Here's another book by Mari Silva that you might like

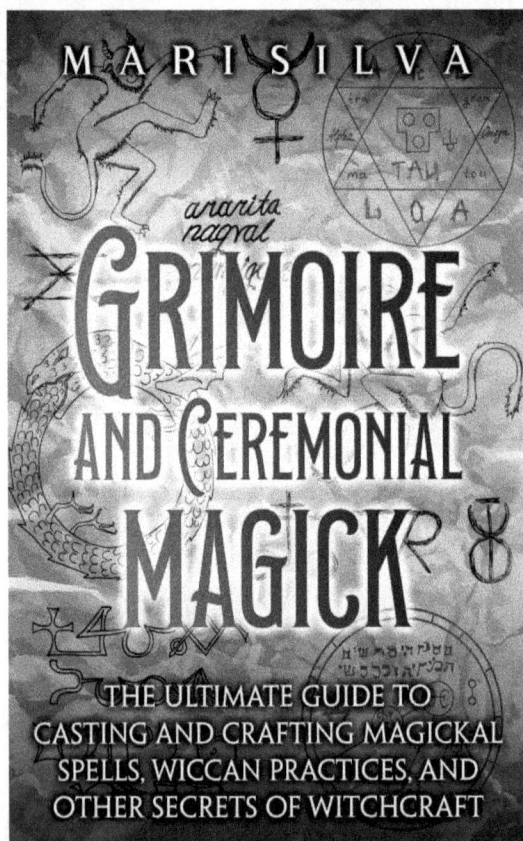

MARI SILVA

anarita nagval

GRIMOIRE AND CEREMONIAL MAGICK

THE ULTIMATE GUIDE TO CASTING AND CRAFTING MAGICKAL SPELLS, WICCAN PRACTICES, AND OTHER SECRETS OF WITCHCRAFT

Your Free Gift

Thanks for downloading this book! If you want to learn more about various spirituality topics, then join Mari Silva's community and get a free guided meditation MP3 for awakening your third eye. This guided meditation mp3 is designed to open and strengthen ones third eye so you can experience a higher state of consciousness.

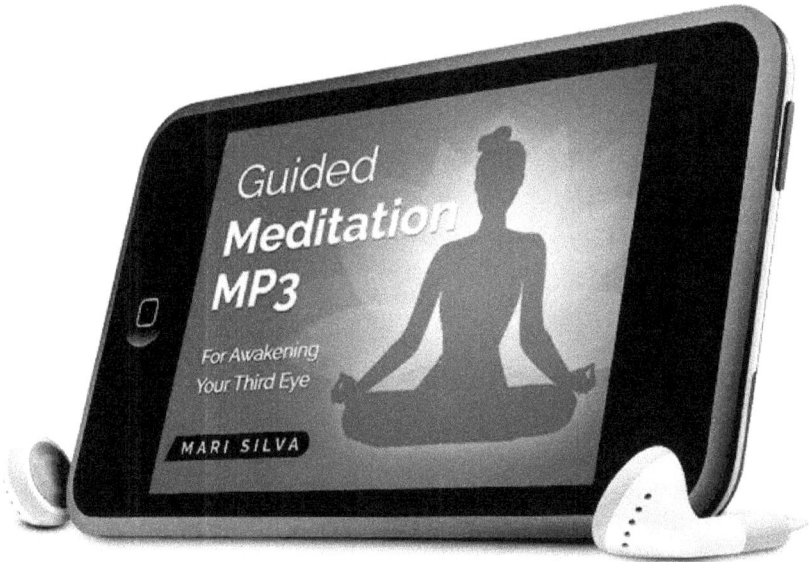

https://livetolearn.lpages.co/mari-silva-third-eye-meditation-mp3

References

"8 Magical Waters: How to Make & Use Moon Water, Sun Water, and More." Otherworldly Oracle, 5 May 2019, https://otherworldlyoracle.com/magical-waters/.

10 Astral Projection Dangers Explained: You Need to Know This | AstralHQ.com. https://astralhq.com/astral-travel-dangers/.

"All about the Five Elements with Rituals." Blog.thewitchsguide.com, 23 July 2021, blog.thewitchsguide.com/all-about-the-five-elements-and-rituals-to-connect/.

"Amulets and Talismans: How to Enchant Jewelry for Protection, Love, Etc." Otherworldly Oracle, 10 July 2019, otherworldlyoracle.com/amulets-talismans-enchant-jewelry/.

"Archangels - Who Are the 17 Archangels and What Is Their Meaning?" Numerology Signs, 4 May 2020, https://numerologysigns.com/archangels/archangels-guide/.

Chabad.org. "What Is Kabbalah? - a Basic Introduction to the Kabbalah." @Chabad, 2 Sept. 2004

Elemental Magick: Fire Spells and Rituals.

"Elementals: What Is an Elemental? And the Guardians of the Watchtowers." Otherworldly Oracle, 1 Dec. 2020, https://otherworldlyoracle.com/elementals-guardians-of-the-watchtowers/.

"Feeling Ungrounded? Here's How to Heal Your Earth Element." YogiApprovedTM, 3 Apr. 2020, www.yogiapproved.com/om/earth-element-healing/.

Frater Samech. "Solomonic Magick - the Key of Solomon the King - the Holy Pentacles." Solomonicmagick.com, 2021

"How to Cast a Magical Circle in 6 Simple Steps." Tess Whitehurst, 19 May 2016, https://tesswhitehurst.com/how-to-cast-a-magical-circle-6-simple-steps/.

How to Consecrate a Witchcraft Tool - Black Witch Coven. 13 Dec. 2020

Kyteler, Emma. Air Element Magick: Elemental Magick for Beginners. https://eclecticwitchcraft.com/air-element/.

"Lesser Banishing Ritual of the Pentagram." Llewellyn.com, 2019, www.llewellyn.com/encyclopedia/article/5139.

"Lesser Ritual of the Hexagram (LRH)." Tryskelion.com, https://tryskelion.com/mag_mag_lesser_ritual_hexagram.html.

LMT, Shanti Dechen, CCAP, CAI. "Grounding and Centering Your Earth Element." Learn-Aroma, 8 Sept. 2020, www.learnaroma.com/single-post/2017/09/14/Grounding-and-Centering-Your-Earth-Element.

"Manifest What You Want from the Universe with Planetary Magick! | Soul and Spirit." Www.soulandspiritmagazine.com

Planetary Magick with Saturn - Black Witch Coven. 20 July 2019.

Polyphanes. "Propitiation Ritual of Saturn." The Digital Ambler, 23 Dec. 2017, https://digitalambler.com/2017/12/23/propitiation-ritual-of-saturn/.

"Protection Magick Basics." Patti Wigington, 1 June 2021.

"Psychic Attacks: 7 Signs and Symptoms to Look For." Www.psychics4today.com, www.psychics4today.com/psychic-attacks/#:~:text=%20The%207%20Signs%20and%20Symptoms%20of%20a.

Skaravaios, Frater. "Middle Pillar Ritual." Into the Aeon, 22 Aug. 2020

"The Fire Elementals – Self-Healing with the Salamanders!" Calista Ascension, 4 Feb. 2012, www.calistaascension.com/fire-elementals-self-healing-salamanders/.

The Magical Keys of Solomon. www.magicalkeysofsolomon.com/.

"The Pentagram Symbol and How to Use It in Your Daily Life." The Witchcraft Way, 29 May 2020, https://welldivined.com/the-pentagram-symbol-and-how-to-use-it/.

"The Rose Cross Ritual - Golden Dawn Document." Hermetics.org, http://hermetics.org/Rose-Cross.html.

Tools in Ceremonial Magick - Black Witch Coven. 10 Feb. 2020.

"What Is Planetary Magick?" Arnemancy, 27 July 2020.

Bucur, Bogdan G. "The Other Clement of Alexandria: Cosmic Hierarchy and Interiorized Apocalypticism.' Vigiliae Christianae 60.3 (2006)

Crowley, Aleister. The Vision and the Voice. Dallas, Tex.: Sangreal Foundation, 1972.

LaVey, Anton S. The Satanic Bible. New York: Avon, 1969.

Michael Knibb, The Ethiopic Book of Enoch: A New Edition in the Light of the Aramaic Dead Sea Fragment (New York: Oxford University Press, 1979).

Regardie, Israel. Enochian Dictionary. Dallas, Tex.: Sangreal Foundation, 1971.

Schueler, Gerald J. An Advanced Guide to Enochian Magic: A Complete Manual for Angelic Magic. St. Paul, Minn.: Llewellyn Publications, 1987.

Turner, Robert. Elizabethan Magic. Londmead, Dorset, England: Element Books, 1989.

Zalewski, Patrick J. Golden Dawn Enochian Magic. St. Paul, Minn.: Llewellyn Publications, 1990

Reed, Annette Yoshiko. "From Asael and Šemiazah to Uzzah, Azzah, and Azael: 3 Enoch 5 (§§ 7-8) and Jewish Reception-History of 1 Enoch.' Jewish Studies Quarterly 8.2 (2001): 105-36. Print.

Suter, David. "Fallen Angel, Fallen Priest: The Problem of Family Purity in 1 Enoch 6 and 20:14;16.' Hebrew Union College Annual 50 (1979): 115-35. Print.

M. Casaubon, A True and Faithful Relation of what passed for many years between Dr. John Dee ... and some spirits (London, 1659).

N. Clulee, John Dee's Natural Philosophy: Between Science and Religion (London, 1988)

D. Harkness, John Dee's Conversations with Angels: Cabala, Alchemy, and the End of Nature (Cambridge, 1999)

W.H. Sherman, John Dee: The Politics of Reading and Writing in the Renaissance (Amherst and Boston, MA, 1995)

G. Szonyi, John Dee's Occultism: Magical Exaltation through Powerful Signs (Albany, NY, 2004)